Minding Your Emotions

Minding Your Emotions

How Understanding Your
Feelings Can Nurture Your Soul

Steve Shores

NAVPRESS

BRINGING TRUTH TO LIFE
P.O. Box 35001, Colorado Springs, Colorado 80935

OUR GUARANTEE TO YOU

We believe so strongly in the message of our books that we are making this quality guarantee to you. If for any reason you are disappointed with the content of this book, return the title page to us with your name and address and we will refund to you the list price of the book. To help us serve you better, please briefly describe why you were disappointed. Mail your refund request to: NavPress, P.O. Box 35002, Colorado Springs, CO 80935.

The Navigators is an international Christian organization. Our mission is to reach, disciple, and equip people to know Christ and to make Him known through successive generations. We envision multitudes of diverse people in the United States and every other nation who have a passionate love for Christ, live a lifestyle of sharing Christ's love, and multiply spiritual laborers among those without Christ.

NavPress is the publishing ministry of The Navigators. NavPress publications help believers learn biblical truth and apply what they learn to their lives and ministries. Our mission is to stimulate spiritual formation among our readers.

ISBN 1-57683-174-4

Cover design by Jennifer Mahalik
Cover illustration by James Wardell / Masterfile
Creative Team: Paul Santhouse, Eric Stanford, Jacqueline Blakely, Laura Spray, Glynese Northam

Some of the anecdotal illustrations in this book are true to life and are included with the permission of the persons involved. All other illustrations are composites of real situations, and any resemblance to people living or dead is coincidental.

Unless otherwise identified, all Scripture quotations in this publication are taken from the *New American Standard Bible* (NASB), © The Lockman Foundation 1960, 1962, 1963, 1968, 1971, 1972, 1973, 1975, 1977, 1995. Other versions used include the *HOLY BIBLE: NEW INTERNATIONAL VERSION®* (NIV®), copyright © 1973, 1978, 1984 by International Bible Society, used by permission of Zondervan Publishing House, all rights reserved; the *New King James Version* (NKJV), copyright © 1979, 1980, 1982, 1990, Thomas Nelson Inc., Publishers; the *Holy Bible, New Living Translation* (NLT), copyright © 1996, used by permission of Tyndale House Publishers, Inc., Wheaton, Illinois 60189, all rights reserved; and the *King James Version* (KJV).

Shores, Steve.
  Minding your emotions : how understanding your feelings can nurture your soul / Steve Shores.
    p. cm.
Includes bibliographical references.
  ISBN 1-57683-174-4
  1. Emotions--Religious aspects--Christianity. I. Title.
BV4597.3 .S55 2002
248.4--dc21   2002002127

Printed in the United States of America
1 2 3 4 5 6 7 8 9 10 / 05 04 03 02

FOR A FREE CATALOG OF
NAVPRESS BOOKS & BIBLE STUDIES,
CALL 1-800-366-7788 (USA)
OR 1-416-499-4615 (CANADA)

To my cherished wife, Susan

Contents

Introduction

Mmay I put in a plug for emotions? Perhaps raise a small cheer for them? Our emotions are an important part of how God made us. We can become healthier, more effective people if we understand our emotions within the context of our total makeup. That, at least, is the premise of this book.

How will my appeal for emotions be heard? One party—let's call them the *subjectivists*—will say, "Oh yeah, baby! Emotions are us! We want to feel and express, feel and express. Let's not go back to that time when we were all shut down, buttoned down, and tightened up. Everyone was hiding, stiff, and formal. Count us in for emotions!" Another party—the *objectivists*—will reply, "You can't trust feelings. What are they? Ephemeral surges of irrationality designed to derail reason. You can't think clearly with a surging or sagging heart. It's too unstable. When reason is fogged by emotions, how are you going to make smart choices?"

Might I venture that neither side has the full story? I want to speak for a third party: the *integrationists*. On behalf of this group, I'd say, "Let's stop this splitting of the human being into fragments—a will over here, a reasoning capacity over there, an imagination off in the corner, an ability to feel way over in the shadows." It's like the old story of the blind men and the elephant: one man encounters an ear and decides that an elephant is like a giant leaf; another one handles the tail and concludes that an elephant is like a rope; and so on all around the animal. Since they don't work together, the blind men can't tell what's in front of them. Similarly, people shatter their concept of a human being into separate pieces: will, reason, imagination, feelings. Let's put those pieces back together again. Scripture portrays the person as a whole, as a unity, as a team of capacities integrated by a longing for God.

In this book I'll concentrate on bringing our emotions out from behind a cloud of suspicion, on one hand, and away from an uncritical expression of all feeling, on the other. I want to help you steer a course between running from your emotions and being run by them. In particular, I will hitch the emotions to the mind. (The will and the imagination are important, too, but we don't have the space here to look closely at how feelings are related to them.) But before we get to the subject of hooking up mind and emotions, let's try to understand the subjectivists and objectivists better.

Subjectivists: Wide-Open Emotions

Novice sailors, instead of harnessing the wind, let themselves be driven before it. They're little more than passengers on a runaway boat. Subjectivists act the same way when the winds of emotion begin to blow. They have no rudder, no keel, no stability. For them, all power is on the side of emotion. They flatten reasoning, will, and imagination.

Subjectivists may tell you that they are honoring the underappreciated capacity of feeling. But in fact they are not honoring their emotions so much as their moods. Later, we'll look in detail at distinctions between mood and emotion. But for now, let me say that mood is vague, unfocused, and defensive, while emotion has the opposite qualities. Furthermore, mood is powerful and intoxicating and can be used to control others ("Leave him alone; he's in one of his moods"). Emotion, on the contrary, does not aim at power over others but at discovery within oneself. As such, emotions can seem overwhelming at first—yet, as we'll see, they can lead us toward deliverance and joy if we mind them properly before God.

Objectivists: Closed-Down Hearts

In a way, the objectivists reflect the Promethean myth. According to early Greek stories, the Titan Prometheus created human beings and made them the greatest of mortal creatures by stealing fire (representing reason) from the sun and giving it to the humans. In the process Prometheus incurred the wrath of Zeus. Like the ancient Greeks, objectivists trust in reason as the savior of humanity.

In fact, the objectivists are impoverished. They regard emotions as if they're vestigial organs, like the appendix. They don't know what to do with emotions, so they shove them aside. Objectivists revere reason so completely that they risk becoming all head and no heart.

Keeping distant from one's emotions versus overindulging in them — this contrast is featured throughout the book. As the title suggests, this book is about bringing mind and emotions together. So we're back to the importance of gaining a proper understanding of the emotions, as created by God.

Closed Heart, Closed Universe

The modern mind has decreed that the physical universe is a closed system and is all that exists. Yet our emotions clamor that this can't be true. Our emotions are malcontents that present contrary findings, evidence for something beyond this so obviously unfulfilled present. Our emotions are longings looking for words, prompting us to find speech and not lapse into silence and numbness, the murder of our souls. When our emotions do find words, we discover (if we listen carefully) that the speech they're looking for is inevitably about hope for something beyond the mere speck of this universe.

The words that our emotions find to speak highlight the gap between the now and the not-yet. The now is unfulfilled. The not-yet brims with God's promise. As God's promise comes from and illuminates the future, so also it comes toward and illuminates the present. It contradicts the present and its tendency to make peace

11

with unfulfillment. Our emotions reflect an unrest in our hearts, a refusal to accept the claim that life must remain unfulfilled. Our emotions are hints of glory, whispers of transcendence, precursors of fulfilled promises, forerunners of the "hope [that] does not disappoint" (Romans 5:5, NIV), and premonitions that God is knocking on the door of this "closed" universe.

Minding our emotions reopens the universe. Philosopher Abraham Heschel puts it this way: "Sometimes we wish the world would cry and tell us about that which made it pregnant with fear-filling grandeur. Sometimes we wish our own heart would speak of that which made it heavy with wonder."[1]

The Emotion Cycle

Emotions make life dance, but only if we let them show us the complexity of our inner selves (most of us are not well acquainted with our insides). Emotions steer us toward the hidden things of the heart.

What kinds of things might be happening within the human? This is where I look to the *emotion cycle,* which consists of a particular sequence:

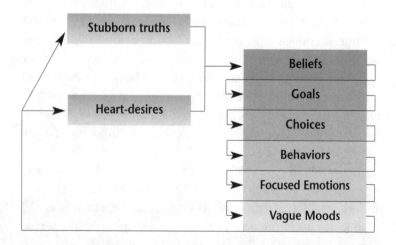

The sequence should be understood with the proviso that, while it moves in the direction indicated by the arrows, each part of the sequence influences every other.

Without the context provided by the emotion cycle, emotions either drain life (because we suppress them) or control life (because we yield to them). We end up emotionally dead (numbness), in a hurricane (chaos), or in a pattern of withdrawal interspersed with explosions of emotion.

But with the context of the cycle (which we'll examine carefully in chapter 4), emotions can lead us not only to wholeness but even to worship. This linkage is displayed time and again in the Psalms. Emotion honestly faced before a loving God becomes worship because feelings show us either our blessedness (joy, gladness, triumph, hope) or our neediness (anger, grief, sadness, fear). If we put these emotions, positive or negative, into a context, rather than truncating them through suppression or indulgence, they shed light on the places in the heart where we are either solidly anchored to God or struggling to climb out of deep pits of unbelief.

In showing how to put emotions into a context, this book presents practical guidance in two parts. The first part lays a groundwork for understanding emotions. It explains what emotions can tell us about ourselves and what it's like to be an emotional being in a difficult world. With that foundation in place, the second part begins building a superstructure of healing by considering some key specific emotions: anger, fear, shame, sadness, joy. Each of these emotions is one that we must learn to "mind" if we are going to be the fully alive people our souls long for us to be.

Part 1

The Nature and Purposes of Emotion

CHAPTER ONE

The Gift of Feelings

Our emotions testify that our deepest desires are no joke.

Our emotional nature has been given to us, along with all our other benefits, for our good by a loving God. Both positive and negative emotions are more valuable to us than we usually recognize. If we'll let them, they'll teach us the truth about ourselves and the One who made us. But facing that truth can be painful and fearful, so suppressing our emotions becomes the order of the day for many of us. What a loss.

Suppressed emotions can't teach us anything. When we bury our feelings, we're like students stuck with a silent teacher: there's no point in going to class. Besides, suppressed emotions, like nearly all buried things, tend to decay. They mingle with other factors to bear distorted offspring that may not resemble our original feelings at all. The original emotions of hurt, sadness, and frustration are transposed into guilt, shame, oppressive pain, anxiety, secondary anger, self-contempt, drivenness, and identity confusion.

Consider the following story.

Donna's Story

Donna is six years old. See her standing there in front of her school, waiting to be picked up? She points a toe at a crack in the sidewalk. She wipes her nose. She scratches the back of her knee where a mosquito got her. She's fidgety because she's hoping for a whopper—that her dad will show up to get her. She hopes the same thing every day. But today, like every day, it's her grandfather who shows up at her school.

She's hurt, sad, and frustrated. She misses her father—misses him like she'd miss being able to breathe. Dimly, she realizes that he's an alcoholic and consequently undependable, but neither that nor anything else excuses him in her mind. He *should* be there. She tells her mother, "I want Daddy to pick me up after school, not Granddad."

Her mother gets angry and says, "You should be grateful that you have your grandfather in your life."

Now Donna feels guilty and confused. Somehow, her longing for her father has been turned into something she's done against her grandfather. She wonders, *What just happened?*

As time passes, Donna receives more rejecting messages from the important people in her life, and her guilt feelings turn into shame. Guilt, we might say, is the feeling that you have *done* something bad; shame is the feeling that you *are* something bad. For Donna, shame becomes pervasive and self-defining, lying around her soul like a sooty cloud, suffocating her. She feels miserable.

But for Donna, guilt and shame represent just the beginnings of her negative feelings and actions. In addition, she has plenty of pain, with no apparent hope for comfort. And anxiety blends into anger: *Why won't comfort come?* Then self-contempt enters her heart: *Only an idiot like me would be unable to find comfort. Everybody else seems to be doing fine.* Then drivenness takes over: *At all costs, I will find comfort.* Soon she becomes compulsive: *Wherever I find comfort, I'll return there over and over.* Identity confusion follows: *I'll go against my design if that helps me find comfort.*

Beginning in adolescence, Donna finds herself drawn to the apparent safety of homosexual relationships. Since she associates the jagged edges of alcohol-induced fatherlessness with the main man in her life, she figures that all men are alike — unreliable and dangerous. The idea of responding deeply to a man is repulsive to her, even though she has been designed by God to do just that. The deeper she becomes involved in lesbianism, the more her gender confusion grows, but she feels it's worth it to fight off the appalling loneliness inside.

Furthermore, Donna's self-against-self conflict and drive to find comfort lead her to seek out friends for support. She attempts to surround herself with lots of people, many of whom are in some sense outcasts, as she feels herself to be. Donna learns that the fastest way to gain companions is through spending money on them — buying them gifts, taking them to dinner, and so forth. She concludes that a lavish lifestyle will win her the friends (that is, comfort) she desperately needs.

For a while, Donna is able to maintain her twin sources of comfort: homosexual relationships and her crowd of outcast friends. She becomes compulsive about returning to both sources. She thinks, *I have to go continually to them; otherwise, I'm comfortless and my pain is overwhelming.* But finally, Donna gets caught. Her high-spending lifestyle leads her to use her job at a bank to open several fraudulent credit accounts, and her superiors find out about it. She also financially defrauds her live-in girlfriend, who kicks her out of their apartment. *Bam!* Just like that, both faucets of comfort are turned off. Her thirsty soul is screaming for water, for comfort. It's time to seek some real help.

In this case, getting help means Donna learns to put her emotions to work *for* her rather than *against* her. No longer suppressed under the stifling of compulsive behaviors, her feelings become servants instead of tyrants; they help her instead of rule her. For example, she begins to see her anxiety in social situations as shedding light on her fear that she'll fail ("act like a geek") in relationships, be rejected, and lose a major supply of comfort. Now she explores her emotions (like anxiety) as budding revelations. What used to be a black hole becomes a candle. As writer Anne Lamott put it about one of her own struggles with anxiety,

"Sitting with all that vulnerability [instead of running from it], I discovered I could ride it."[1] Likewise, Donna can be carried along by the energy of facing what's real instead of suppressing it and turning it into a destructive force in her life.

Falsehoods About Feelings

Clearly, in Donna's story I'm highlighting not only the wisdom that can come through emotions but also the danger of dismissing them and losing out on the light they might bring. Suppressed emotions doom us to walking in the dark. Dismissing our emotions is like throwing away flashlights during a power outage.

Sad to say, humans are resourceful at discarding their feelings. We have several strategies for throwing our emotions away. Three of the most common ones come out when we say that emotions are for weaklings, that emotions are evidence of instability, and that emotions are less important than reason.

Emotions Are for Weaklings

A prime falsehood people accept in order to discount emotion is that giving in to feelings is a sign of weakness. The high value placed on personal strength becomes an excuse for escaping the risks associated with emotion. As we'll see in a bit, women have their own way of expressing this lie. But men are especially big on this one, having been bred (so it seems) for toughness.

Deep inside, every man feels that, to be a real man, he should be able to take a bullet without making a sound, work around the clock without taking a break, and hear the most devastating news without dropping a tear. He should be able to defend his loved ones with wit and muscle. He should be able to win whenever he competes. He should never show weakness, never give up. If you remember the story of G. Gordon Liddy sticking his finger into a candle flame without flinching, you know what I mean.

Actually, though, God designed men to be courageous, not tough. The differences between courage and toughness may seem slight, but they're really quite striking. One difference is that courage is easily compatible with relationships, while toughness is not. Courage exists for the sake of others; toughness generates pride and isolation. Courage wants to care; toughness wants to be admired from a distance. Courage is compatible with vulnerability; toughness denies all weakness. Courage is Jesus on the cross; toughness is Peter slicing off Malchus's ear with a sword. You get the idea.

God made men to be courageous in the midst of their emotions. Courage is willing to endure the pain of learning from emotions, for it is informed by wisdom, which assures that the pain will resolve itself into new light and growth. Toughness, on the other hand, can't handle the stress of learning from emotion. Toughness is really rather weak.

Imagine a man who, a week after triple-bypass surgery, is back at work for half-days. A week after that, he's at work full time and planning to get back into his hobby, horseback riding. All of this goes against medical advice. Ask him why he's pushing himself, and you'll hear, "Why should I let some doctor with soft hands and, for all I know, a soft head, tell me what to do?"

As our tough guy pushes himself unwisely, he fails to detect the niggle of fear in his heart about his own mortality. So he requires his wife to deny her fear as well, and she becomes outwardly pleasant in a plastic way but doesn't show her real self. Both people are reduced to automatons, compulsively fighting off a fear that would, if faced, make them more human. It's hard for them to be wise because neither allows the openness that begets wisdom.

Western culture has lost a whole treasury of wisdom because of its tendency toward reductive thinking. For example, when people are viewed as mere machines, as with the couple above, it becomes easier to reduce the meaning of life to personal pleasure. How can such a worldview accommodate wisdom—or, for that matter, the courage it takes to persevere in life long enough to develop that wisdom?

A worldview that reduces the meaning of life to pleasure favors the young, for they are the most adept at seizing it. The old, then, get short shrift. Yet it is the old who are most likely to have been schooled by life. The wisdom bank of a culture imbued by such a worldview becomes more and more depleted.

Without wisdom, there is a dearth of big-picture thinking — the very thinking necessary to delay gratification and build relationships that are more than brief exercises in narcissism. Without relational depth, life degenerates into desperate self-aggrandizement (desperate because there are many pigs and few troughs). Made into a competition, life becomes painful and lonely. Toughness is highly valued because it supplies a sense of invulnerability in a harsh world. But as we've seen, the male ideal of toughness does not deliver what it promises.

The premium on toughness amounts to a confession by men that they've given up on cultivating relationships. So the responsibility for maintaining relationships falls on women. Meanwhile, though, women have their own problems with relationships.

Women tend to gravitate toward stoicism rather than toughness. An outward pleasantry and politeness turns out to be a veneer over a steel core. That core is organized around a commitment to avoid seeming needy. This commitment often coexists with a Pollyannaish denial of the harsher realities of life. Stoicism, then, has a dishonest streak: it can't admit how hard life really is in a fallen world.

It turns out that stoicism and toughness, not emotions, are for weaklings.

Emotions Are Evidence of Instability

Many people think that showing any sign of emotion marks one as unstable, not to be trusted. Therefore, they reason, it's better for them to keep their emotions strictly in check.

Actually, emotions are evidence of instability only for those who are *ruled* by their emotions. When an emotion instantly takes hold of someone's behavior, we could call that person *reactive* — that is, his emotions provoke immediate actions instead of calm reflection. In the following exchange between a dating couple, it becomes clear who is reactive.

JENNIFER: Tyler, I feel that sometimes, when we're trying to have a discussion, you just attack me from out of the blue. I don't even know I've said anything wrong, and you're all over me.

TYLER: Oh, so you think I'm attacking you, climbing all over you. Well, I know how we can solve that! I'll just stop talking with you. If you can't let me talk without accusing me of attacking, maybe we should just not see each other anymore!

JENNIFER: I'm not saying you always attack. There are just times when I'm surprised by how intense things get, and I didn't even see it coming.

TYLER: I can't believe you. Why haven't you told me this before? I'm not willing to be characterized as the jerk in this relationship. If I have to worry about your feelings being attacked every time I talk with you, what's the point?

Clearly, Tyler is feeling something so overwhelming that he can't slow down long enough to reflect on why his inner anxiety has skyrocketed. Rather than doing the internal work to understand the anxiety, he is placing the burden on Jennifer, making *her* work hard to explain herself in just the right way to defuse the anxiety.

In fact, anyone who is ruled by emotions makes everyone around him work harder. His relationships suffer because everyone around him is so tired of the extra labor it takes to make him feel OK. Prescription: if you're in a relationship with a "reactor," resist the temptation to work so hard to keep him OK. Encourage him to do the internal work himself instead of shifting the burden to you.

Emotions themselves, then, are *not* evidence of instability. It would be better to say that those who react immediately to their emotions tend to be unstable. These folks have never learned how to place a buffer between themselves and their emotions. The buffer is the skill of reflection that involves taking advantage of the human ability to think about what we're feeling. Because feelings are interpretable, we might say that our feelings are a part of us that are out there looking for words to express themselves. They are undirected sensations looking for a compass. We can properly express them when we identify the factors underneath them and put them into words.

Reactive people are not finding the right words for their emotions. Sometimes they don't reach for words at all; they turn their emotions directly into actions. This is called *acting out*. For example, a person who, upon feeling a hint of emotional pain, automatically opens the refrigerator to get something to eat (subconsciously hoping to bury the negative feeling with a physical pleasure) is acting out. The gift of words is completely gone. This person is overlooking whole substrata of factors that intervene between emotion and behavior. Emotions become behavior—*wham!*—just like that. Road rage is a good example of this abrupt maneuver. Is it any wonder that we live in an increasingly uncivil world?

Silence, too, can be a form of reactivity. There are those who deem it a virtue to be a man or woman of few words. But silence can't be automatically good if words are a gift from God. In fact, silence is often the reaction of withdrawal, a refusal to participate. Silence can be eloquently punitive speech. One who converts his emotions directly into silence is acting out as much as is the patroller of the refrigerator.

I've had to learn about the misuse of silence in my own life. For most of my life, whenever I felt pain, I'd withdraw from others to work it out on my own. If life handed me a thousand-piece puzzle, I'd smile bravely, exit inside myself, and try to put the thing together without help and without the picture on the puzzle box. What did this get me? A lot of unfinished puzzles and confused relationships. Now I've learned that if another person really cares about me, he or she will be interested in the pain I feel. Imagine: over the years, I'd come to accept that love would somehow include the other's *not* caring about my pain! My silences when in pain were my defenses against what I assumed was indifference. Many times, my assumption was wrong—others *did* care.

Of course, not all silences are defensive. Some silences consist of a prudent seeking for the right words. Some silences are an admission that the right words can't yet be found and that waiting for them is the only wise policy. Some silences are even prayerful—a seeking of a word from God. Silence can also be contemplative, a searching for the real essence of a person or situation. My point, therefore, is not to criticize all silence but to sensitize us to the kind of silence that is punitive and selfish. An honest, open dealing with emotion is not a sign of instability but of stability and strength.

Emotions Are Less Important Than Reason

Sometimes people see emotions as a lower order of human capacity than reason. Yes, I have emotions, they may think, but they lead me astray. So I'd better keep my feelings firmly subordinated to my thinking.

Actually, ranking the elements of humans (intellect, emotion, will, imagination) is not a biblical idea. All these capacities are God-given and equally important. The removal of any one of them is a serious loss. They are meant to work in concert, with no jockeying for position.

The concept of ranking human capacities comes from the ancient Greeks, who valued reason above all. For example, Plato taught that only the mind—not the body or the soul—was immortal. The biblical view of man, on the other hand, sees every God-given aspect of humanity (in other words, every aspect except sin) as vital. The Bible knows nothing of an exalted mind and devalued emotions. Yet the suspicion that our feelings are inherently shameful remains widespread.

In a recent counseling session I was trying to get behind the façade of a man who struggles with alcoholism. As I approached him with how it felt for me and others to be on the receiving end of his continual "sales pitch" persona, he recoiled and said, "What do you want me to do, show you my soft underbelly?" He was incredulous.

I returned with "Yes, exactly. The soft parts, the emotional parts, the hurting parts — these are the parts of you that you're so ashamed of but that are much more inviting than the sales pitch."

He followed that with "But I've been told all my life that emotions put you at a disadvantage."

This man must have grown up with some unsafe people. Yet many of us can identify with him. We, too, have been told that the emotional side of the human is inferior.

The truth is, far from being inferior, our emotions are essential to our overall self-understanding. Our capacity to feel is like an early warning system calling us toward a level of awareness we don't normally enter. Emotions invite us to gain access to the deeper parts of our hearts. Emotions tell us that there is a depth inside that longs for more than can be provided by this world. When we're cut off from our emotions, we're separated from the yearning that makes us human.

What is this yearning? It is a thirst for a nobility and a splendor that lie beyond the human plane and that catch us up into grandeur. This "catching up" we instinctively know to be a home-coming. This world, we sense, is not our true home. Something inside us has become small, cramped, selfish. God wants to cleanse us and make us pure. He wants to set us a large place, love us, and receive us with generous gifts. First we are to be made right. Then we are to be led homeward. Only this can answer our yearning hearts. Only this can bring a hope large enough to rest in. Abraham Heschel comments, "Man's true fulfillment depends upon communion with that which transcends him. The cure of the soul begins with a *sense of embarrassment,* embarrassment at our pettiness, prejudices, envy, and conceit; embarrassment at the profanation of life. A world that is full of grandeur has been converted into a carnival."[2]

What reason and the other aspects of our humanness cannot do for us, our emotions can. They are secondary in no way. They alone reveal our transcendent yearning.

Yes and No

The connection between our yearning and our emotion is so important that it is worth exploring further. Let's divide our emotional experiences into up and down emotions. The up emotions include joy, excitement, gladness, and contentment. The down emotions include anger, sorrow, despair, anxiety, and fear. The up emotions cluster around experiences of fulfillment, satisfaction, meaning, and purpose. The down emotions are concentrated around times of disappointment, uncertainty, loss, threat, pain, and hopelessness. Another way to put it is this: The up emotions well up within us when life has said yes to us in some important way. The down emotions emerge when life has said no to something important to us.

At the deepest level of our being, we are made for yes, not no. Does this mean that we can demand yeses all our lives? It does not. Remember that cramped, selfish part of us? There are times when that self-seeking, tantrum-throwing piece of our hearts needs to hear no in order to be prepared for a greater yes. Still, we are not, all in all, designed for a steady diet of no.

Our up emotions suggest to us that, just maybe, there is a yes that will utterly, delightfully fill and complete us. We intensely hope that this yes is real and will finally quench our inner thirst. Our down emotions indicate that we have encountered a significant no, and this makes us fear that the wondrous yes will never reach us. Our up emotions remind us that we're made to live in hope. Our down emotions remind us that hopelessness is toxic to us and that there must be a yes beyond the tidal surges of no in this world. Is there a hope that won't disappoint us?

Let's look at this yes-no interplay in a real-life scenario.

Killer Headache

Recently, I awoke at three in the morning with a tremendous, debilitating headache. Usually I can shake these off with a couple of aspirin, but this one had grabbed me like a tiger grabs its victim. Throbbing radiated all over my head to the point that, by six o'clock in the morning, I was nauseated and threw up. No painkillers touched this headache, and yet I had to go to work. The thought of counseling folks when I was overwhelmed with my own bodily anguish made me feel anger and self-pity. I can hear you saying, "Just take the day off! What's the big deal?" At the time, though, I was living on a financial edge. I couldn't afford to cancel a whole day of appointments. This made me feel ashamed. I heard a voice in my head speaking to this effect: You see? I told you that you were inept. Others your age have company-provided sick days or have set aside enough money for an emergency fund. If anyone knew about your financial bind, they'd laugh out loud. My emotions were running the negative gamut: anger, fear, shame, pride, self-pity, despair. As Anne Lamott says, "Sometimes, my mind is like a bad neighborhood. I try not to go there too often."[3]

Life had said a big no in the form of crummy health and an impossible bind: work when I couldn't work. This no dragged out into the open my fears of being inept at providing for my family. The no reminded me that I can't live long in the neighborhood of negativity. I desperately needed a sustaining yes to come tearing toward me out of the darkness. Sometimes those yeses come through people who love me; sometimes through nature; sometimes through the works of great authors; sometimes through music. This time, as at other times, I found my yes in the words of Scripture. I read in the Bible that "momentary, light affliction is producing for us an eternal weight of glory far beyond all comparison" (2 Corinthians 4:17).

I found my yes in the idea that, for the believing soul (that is, the soul resting in Christ), affliction produces unimaginable splendor. This splendor waits beyond the "momentary" bad stuff, which is lightweight by comparison — that is, affliction is limited to the now and will have no place in the not-yet. Moreover, affliction is a feather compared to the coming splendor, which is so substantial as to have a "weight." And in some mysterious way, for the believing soul there is a productive link between present affliction and deferred splendor. I found my yes in the blessed thought that life's afflictions will not go to waste, that affliction can never be used to argue that life is meaningless. Someday, according to the promise of Scripture, affliction will be turned into an obedient creature whose job will be to weave together skeins of glory in which I will be wrapped as in a splendid robe. This exalted yes brought healing to the broken places caused by the demoralizing no I'd heard that day.

How to Find a Yes

When no overtakes us, we have three options: suppress it, be controlled by it, or listen to it and find a countering yes. On the day of my killer headache, there were times when I was controlled by the no. The no was driving me, and I couldn't find the skill or wisdom to make this fierce wind work in my favor. I was blown off course. But after a grave struggle, there was a moment of grace. There was a realization, a crystal clarity like that found in Gerard Manley Hopkins's poem "That Nature is a Heraclitean Fire and of the comfort of the Resurrection." The relevant lines are these:

All is in an enormous dark
Drowned. O pity and indignation! Manshape, that shone
Sheer off, disseveral, a star, death blots black out; nor mark
Is any of him at all so stark
But vastness blurs and time beats level. Enough! the Resurrection,
A heart's-clarion! Away grief's gasping, joyless days, dejection.
Across my foundering deck shone
A beacon, an eternal beam. Flesh fade, and mortal trash
Fall to the residuary worm; world's wildfire, leave but ash:
In a flash, at a trumpet crash,
I am all at once what Christ is, since he was what I am, and
This Jack, joke, poor potsherd, patch, matchwood, immortal diamond,
Is immortal diamond.

On a day of almost perfect wretchedness, my "deck" *was* badly foundering. I had almost capsized, like the psalmist who said, "As for me, I'd almost completely lost my footing. I saw that the polluted, the perverse, the dishonest, and the betrayers were getting ahead and prospering" (I'm paraphrasing Psalm 73:2-9 here). But God *did* send "a beacon, an eternal beam." Whether we think of our boat turning over in a dark sea or of losing our footing on treacherous terrain, the need is the same: to hear a great, sustaining yes from a source beyond our own hearts or minds. And God, who is a speaking God, is generously inclined to reach us with his yes.

When life says no, our emotions are designed to tell us: "Look, you will find this world too small for your greatest desire. Let this no remind you that this setback, though painful and maybe agonizing, is a clue to your real nature. You are made for heaven, and you don't yet live there. It's a painful bind of which this no is stark evidence. But it also whispers to you about hope. The no is saying, 'Don't look to yourself to find a yes that will counter this disappointment. Look to God, who alone knows the yes, the final affirmation, that is mighty enough to overwhelm this no and all others.'"

Our yes emotions also have a message for us: "You see, I told you that home is up ahead! So don't focus on generating another yes for yourself. Otherwise, you'll become compulsive. Enjoy the yes, but don't fixate on it. Instead, work on knowing the One who gave the yes. Be still, relax, know him. Then all manner of things will be well."

Two Cautions

Like a general understanding of anything, this view of yes and no emotions needs to be tidied up a bit when it comes to specific cases. Two such cases come immediately to my mind.

First, those of us who have a melancholy temperament need to guard against a tendency to fall in love with the noes. Melancholics can become like Eeyore in the Winnie-the-Pooh stories. Remember him? He was the downcast donkey with the low, monotone voice. Always predicting disaster, he seemed to want defeat to be snatched from the jaws of victory. Life says enough noes as it is. Yet melancholics tend to discover the mother lode of negativity, sink a mine shaft to it, and dig there forever. A wise prayer for the melancholic, then, might be, "Lord, help me to detect those times when I'm more negative than life is. Help me to see what I might be getting from living, as it were, on the dark side of the moon. What is it about joy that makes me skittish? You tell me to be joyful, because you're throwing a party. Help me not to beg off (as usual) and go to work in the kitchen in a morose funk. Teach me to sense your smile upon me. May the light of that smile pierce the gloom I have carried and nourished for so long."

Second, people with a self-serving bent might think it OK to grab, on their own terms, all the yeses they can find. Granted, there's no shortage of ways to latch on to yeses. But most of them are short-term and come with a hidden price tag. Grasping behavior generates only artificial yeses that inevitably deteriorate into an enormous no. Sometimes our down emotions are telling us that our heart is sick of phony yeses. We may need to ask ourselves, *Why aren't the yeses I've heard in life more satisfying? Why do I need another one so soon?* A yes that doesn't satisfy may be no more than a self-induced high — poor fare for a hungry heart.

That last phrase, *a hungry heart,* gets us back to the meat of this chapter: we have a God-given gift to feel, and that gift, while it may lead us along some harrowing valleys, is a guide to the heights, where we find that our deepest desires are no joke. On those high places we discover that our desires are like a code that makes no sense until it is matched with something else — in this case, the outpoured love of God. His love decodes our desires until we understand that, all along, our deepest feelings — both good and bad — are really our heart's clamoring that we're terribly homesick. We notice that our feelings, if we'll listen to them with a sensitive ear, are calling out for a home that we ourselves can neither make nor find. In this sense, our feelings — our much disparaged feelings — are closely akin to prayer.

CHAPTER 2

The Denied Heart

To many, emotions are the "untouchables" of
the human makeup.

I n societies where a rigid caste system is in place, high-caste
individuals will carefully avoid any member of the lowest
social classes, man, woman, or child. They'll sweep even the
hems of their garments away from these "untouchables" so as not
to "pollute" themselves by coming into contact with them. Ideas
of "better" and "worse" people are so firmly fixed in the minds of
members of the upper classes that they shun those "below" them.

We condemn such snobbish snubbing when it is practiced in
an external way by others. Yet many of us are guilty of similar
attitudes — in this case, not about others (though that may be
true as well) but about aspects of our own selves. We've made a
caste system of the human makeup, assigning reason the highest
place and leaving emotions clinging to the bottom rung.
Emotions are the "untouchables" for the typical American
Christian. They might pollute us, we imagine. So we regard them
as an inconvenience we must tolerate until we get to heaven, a
sort of hangnail of the heart.

If that kind of thinking is on target, then we'd expect God likewise to diminish emotions. Does he? And if not, what purpose did
he have in mind when making us emotional beings?

The Emotional Life of Deity

I believe Christians who treat emotions as "untouchables" will get a big surprise when they arrive in God's kingdom. There they will find—emotions! Imagine their astonishment at encountering a God who feels deeply, suffers profoundly, and scales the heights of joy. Their limited view of God will have to be unfurled like a sail before the wind. They'll realize that emotions are not the result of humanity's fall into sin when they enter a realm where "the morning stars sang together and all the sons of God shouted for joy" at God's creation (Job 38:7). They'll know they must reorder their heads when they find themselves present in a place where "there is joy in the presence of the angels of God over one sinner who repents" (Luke 15:10).

"OK," I hear a skeptic interposing, "maybe angels get carried away every so often while God stays above it all. Angels might be irrepressible, jolly, fat cherubs who rollick around heaven while God rolls his eyes and exudes stately indifference from his lofty throne." In other words, God himself is emotionless, even though he allows emotions from the spirit servants in his heaven.

Is the skeptic right? Over the years, some theologians have thought so. There was a time when the church's best thinkers insisted that God was "apathetic" ("without emotions," unmoved by anything outside himself). But they did not derive that idea from the Bible. Rather, it seeped into the church from Greek philosophies, primarily that of Aristotle, who said, "Friendship occurs where love is offered in return. But in friendship with God there is no room for friendship to be offered in return, indeed there is not even room for love. For it would be absurd for anyone to assert that he loved Zeus."[1] While Christian thinkers never went this far regarding the God of the Bible, for a while they occupied themselves with developing different views of God's disinterestedness.

Today, belief in God's apathy is rightly out of favor in the theological world, yet it continues to resonate in popular Christian thought. It's fair to say the Christian view of God is still infected with Greek concepts like God's being dispassionate about our plight. Too often, we think of him as sitting in splendid aloofness, a detached observer of the human drama.

I was recently talking with a counselee who had just gotten terrible news about her health. After some discussion, I said, "I think God is sad for you."

She replied, "I've never thought of God as being sad."

Is God an emotional being? In his study of the Old Testament prophets, Abraham Heschel has answered with a passionate "Yes!" When God wanted to portray his longing to reclaim Israel, he commanded Hosea to marry a faithless woman, as God had "married" a faithless nation, Israel. Heschel says that the Old Testament prophet "discloses *a divine pathos* [a deep willingness to be affected by those whom God loves], not just a divine judgment. The pages of the prophetic writings are filled with echoes of divine love and disappointment, mercy and indignation. The God of Israel is never impersonal."[2]

What does this mean for you and me in the strange storminess of everyday living? It means that God adds his tears to our own. It means that he is touched by our suffering and touches us with his passionate, caring response. It means that there are times when his heart "is turned over within [him]" in his agony and "all [his] compassions are kindled" (Hosea 11:8).

You may never have pictured the kindling wood in God's heart catching fire for you. Maybe you can relate to my counselee, never having thought of God as being sad about your problems or feeling any emotion toward you. If so, at this point it might help you to stop and pray this prayer:

> Lord, could it really be that your feelings are aflame toward me when I'm struggling, hurting, ashamed, confused, doubtful, defeated? Do you really care about me that much? I know you died for me in Jesus, but sometimes I've allowed his death to be just another fact-on-file. Help me to see that the Cross is evidence of your feeling, that it's

not just a factual datum but the conquering intensity of your love. May the Cross no longer be to me a lonely event of the past but instead a sign of your commitment to me, of your loyal love, of your heart being turned upside-down on my behalf, of your coming after me until I'm caught up into your arms. Amen.

This prayer introduces two theological categories that help us understand God's emotion: the covenant and the Cross.

God cares about us because he made a covenant with us. He has bound himself to a commitment in which he receives all who will put their lives in his hands, and his heart is tied up in how people respond to that commitment. God has bound himself to us; the fact that we matter to him is welded into his nature. God has linked himself with us in an unbreakable relationship. He has pledged his heart forever.

The idea of God's covenant implies that what affects us affects him. The bond is intimate, close, personal. When God looks at you, his heart does a flip-flop. God *responds*. His concern and power join together over you. You make an impact on him. He gets emotional. He gets passionate. Actually, he *stays* passionate just by nature. Why? Because he is love and because he loves what and who he has made.

In that mighty, relentless love, he's determined to reclaim his creation from the Devil, smashing sin, death, and hell in the process. Now you see why the angels dance with joy when even one sinner repents. They're happy because their Leader and Master has restored another heart, sealing it off from the power of death and sin. Another child is safe! And they're happy because their Lord is happy; their joy is the joy of the Lord.

The Cross is God's risk on our behalf. Because he desired to make a new covenant with us, he exposed his Son to the blows of death. We are gravely mistaken when we view the Cross as simply the "next step" in God's plan of salvation. Some Christians imagine the Father, at the time of Christ's ministry on earth, as thinking, *OK, the Jews have failed to be a kingdom of priests, then we had a big exile over that, then there was a four-hundred-year coffee break between the testaments. Now the Jews have failed to recognize their Messiah, so according to my master blueprint, it's time for Jesus to die on the cross.* That's not the way he thinks. The Cross is not a "step" but a magnificent plunge into shame and battle, into humiliation and heartache, into abandonment and Godforsakenness, into death and chaos. The Cross is a burning sign of God's wild, reckless love for us.

The atmosphere of heaven *is* emotional. It's an atmosphere of joy and suffering, striving and passion, delight and wrath. The suffering in heaven stems from the awareness that, as yet, all has not been made right. The striving in heaven occurs as the whole of God's kingdom focuses on making things right. The wrath in heaven is against those agents who resist the kingdom's effort to make things right. A pretty dynamic place, wouldn't you say? Heart stirrings are erupting all over! By comparison, we earthlings — with our shallow feelings, anemic joys, passing rages, petty vindictiveness, uncertain smiles, and fitful addictions — are a bland lot. And our failure to understand the purpose of the emotions God has given to us humans (the only earthly creatures made in the emotional God's image) is nothing short of tragic.

Emotion As a Barometer

Getting to know God as an emotional being shows that emotions are not, in and of themselves, marks of immaturity. But we know that an individual has jumped to such a conclusion when she says things like "Oh, you know her; she's just emotional" or "Her emotions got the better of her." We may secretly judge an emotional person to be unstable. Within ourselves we may make this judgment: He's just not stable. But what we may really mean is, He's not like me — stoic.

Our discomfort with whatever is unlike us smacks of an arrogance that says, Anyone who wants to connect with me should be like me. Unemotional people seem to think everyone should resemble the character Spock on the old Star Trek series, deliberately suppressing all emotion. One man asked me, "Why can't my wife just let these things roll off her back like I do?" It turned out that "these things" were issues like financial irresponsibility on his part. Her pained response at his landing them in oceans of debt was completely normal. If he had used her pain as a messenger, he might have learned compassion, humility, and repentance. Sometimes, being unemotional is a mark of immaturity.

When we say casually, "How are you doing?" and the other person's response reflects honest struggle, we might pull away from that person a bit. We don't want to know how that person is really doing; we just want to hear the standard "I'm fine." That may in part be the case because we're in a hurry, but it's usually because we're uncomfortable with emotional turmoil and suffering. We think, *I wonder what that person's doing wrong?* I guess the answer might be "The same things the psalmists were doing wrong," since the Psalms throb with emotional upheaval.

Another mistaken response to emotions is to interpret them as signs of weakness. Many times, I've heard counselees exclaim, "If only I could get rid of these feelings!" My response? "You might as well try to get rid of your heart." Feelings are a part of who we are. We can't excise them from us like a diseased organ. Nor should we want to: they serve important purposes that reason, will, and imagination cannot. Troubling feelings, for example, are valuable to us because they are evidence of . . . well, trouble.

If our emotions are telling us of a problem inside, shouldn't we ask ourselves, *What is the problem?* But too often we don't. Instead of treating our emotions as messengers, we either use them as fuel and are consciously driven by them ("I can't help it; that's just the way I feel!") or we shove them away and are subconsciously controlled by them. We either chuck the problem into our internal gunnysack or we spray our emotions all over ourselves or someone else. Either way, our motivation is distorted. We're driven by emotions into selfishness rather than being enticed by them toward God.

I would suggest this alternative to both the conscious and the subconscious misuse of emotions: interpret your emotion as your God-given internal barometer. Just as a barometer measures changes in air pressure, *emotions indicate changes in the relationship between our personal story and the realities of the external world.*

I think that the italicized sentence is crucial. Let's look it over by breaking it in two.

Emotions Indicate Something About Our Personal Story

Everyone is living within a story. Or, as I like to put it, every life has themes, dreams, and schemes. Our emotions have a big influence in these parts of our personal story.

As we discuss personal stories, let's remember that each one is unique. As an example, one person's story might include this theme-dream-scheme set:

▶ *Theme* — I'm always getting in trouble somehow.
▶ *Dream* — I dream of a world where people don't jump to conclusions about me, where people understand me.
▶ *Scheme* — I'll punish the people who I perceive are quick to judge me. I'll appeal my case to people who seem to understand me.

Can't relate to that set? Here's another example:

▶ *Theme* — I've always felt small and helpless.
▶ *Dream* — I dream of a world where I'm the man, where people respect and fear me.
▶ *Scheme* — I'll project a macho, invulnerable image that intimidates others.

Your sets won't be quite like either of these two examples. But do you get the idea of every person living out a story with themes, dreams, and schemes? And do you sense the significance of our understanding the story in which we're living?

For example, if I'm often angry, I may be telling myself a story in which I see others as constantly interfering with my goals. If I'm anxious much of the time, I may be telling myself a story in which I'm always small and the rest of the world is large and overwhelming. If I'm sad a lot, I may be telling myself a story in which loss is normal and gain is abnormal.

Our emotions, if we pay attention and read them with Scripture-fed wisdom, are there to help us understand our story.

Emotions Indicate Something About the Realities of the World

The outside world doesn't stop to adjust to our personal story. The world doesn't take our themes, dreams, and schemes into account. So unless we're prepared to retreat into unreality, we have to take our story into account, and our emotions can help us do that.

To understand how this works, let's consider the case of a man who has the following story set:

▶ *Theme* — I've often felt unnoticed and unimportant.
▶ *Dream* — I dream of a world where I'm the center of attention.
▶ *Scheme* — I'm willing to work for this attention, so I'll figure out how to attract it.

Some days, as this person encounters the stream of people and events in his life, he finds that the conditions are conducive to his getting a lot of attention. "Yeah!" he says, and his heart is filled with up emotions. But other days, the people-and-events stream is brutally indifferent to his quest for attention. He feels ignored, shoved aside, even abandoned. His heart is flooded with down emotions. The world is impinging negatively on his personal story, and it hurts.

The same thing happens to each of us, regardless of the nature of our personal story. The world of everyday relationships and events, the world of the social and schedule flow, has its own momentum, over which we have little control. Every day, therefore, individual stories encounter this massive *people-and-events stream,* as I have called it, especially as it connects with them through the scheme aspect of their personal story. Our emotions reflect whether the people-and-events stream is allowing us to advance our story in the way we want it to go or whether it is blocking our intent.

Sometimes the world cooperates with the scheme we've cooked up to make our story have the happy ending we've imagined. Our emotions reflect this, and we feel happy, up, contented. But this is not necessarily a good situation. Odd that I'd say that, isn't it? I mean, most of us are striving to get life to line up with our internal plan for happiness, right? And when life finally lines up with our plan, we *should* be happy, right? Not necessarily.

Hold that thought, because first I want to introduce another angle on our discussion.

There are times when the people-and-events stream decidedly does *not* cooperate with our scheme for bending life toward our happy ending. Instead, life takes its own stubborn course. Fertility treatments don't work, let's say. Or the biological mother doesn't show up for the first-time meeting her child has set up. Or the random fall you experienced brings chronic, excruciating pain. Or a beloved child ends up on drugs. Or a spouse says, "I've had an affair." Our emotions reflect such obstacles, and we feel down, enraged, crushed. But this is not necessarily a bad situation. Those, too, are odd words, aren't they? Loss is loss, isn't it? Shouldn't loss bring pain? Yes and no.

Let's see why certain forms of happiness can be bad while certain forms of loss and disappointment can be good. Consider the following intertwined stories.

Jack and Sally's Stories

Jack, a man now in his forties, grew up in an unemotional, rule-bound, controlling family. His mother was especially strict, constantly bringing him back in line through her coldness, distance, and disapproval. During those years, a repeating theme in Jack's story was his being tormented by the straitjacket his family placed on him. For example, he wanted to go to law school, but his mother talked him out of it. He chafed at this but went into the business world, where he ended up unsuccessful. Jack began to dream of a world where he was free, unconfined, unfettered. He schemed to create this world. As he grew more and more bitter about business losses and marital discord, he became willing to sacrifice ever more to gain his freedom. Ultimately, Jack left his wife and family to marry the woman with whom he'd been having an affair. At last, he felt happy. Life, finally, had lined up with his dream of freedom.

Is this a good situation? Let's examine it. And to do so, first let's see what became of Jack's ex-wife, Sally.

Her father had quit school at fourteen to work because his father was an alcoholic who didn't support his family. The theme in this family group, handed down from generation to generation, was that the family must stay rigidly close or else it will fall apart. Sally's dream, then, was about a nuclear family blended closely with her extended family, especially with her parents. In her scheme, every holiday and Sunday and special occasion would be a time to do homage to her extended family. Another part of her scheme was that she and her family would continue the tradition of looking good in the community, thus cleansing the shame of her grandfather's alcoholism. So, when her husband divorced her, he shattered her dream as he actualized his own. Is this a bad situation?

The answer depends on whether Sally can find a more complete story that embraces the good elements of her previous story (for example, a high view of family) *and* helps her let go of its unhealthy aspects (for example, fear of shame leading to suffocating closeness). But it's unlikely that she will search for a better story unless she can face what she really believes — that is, face the real beliefs and values that run her life. These beliefs and values emerge from the impact of her life's story thus far. Sally's story has both formed and deformed her. How can she discover what is healthy and what is diseased in her? By learning from her emotions. Her situation is bad, but it will stay bad only if she doesn't learn from it. Her emotions are there to help her learn.

The same is true of the man who divorced her. Jack feels happy, but as we asked earlier, is this a good situation? Even apart from the Bible's disapproval of adultery and divorce, this man's situation is not a good one unless he, like his ex-wife, can find a more complete story. Jack needs a conclusion that affirms the good aspects of his story (his longing for freedom, his hatred of being controlled) while exposing the bad (his lack of courage, his failure to extricate his wife from the mesh of her family). Like Sally, Jack must learn how his story has formed and deformed him. He, too, must learn from his emotions.

Well, then, how *does* someone learn from his or her emotions? There are three ways: First, by realizing that emotions, especially strong ones, signal a change in the way the outside world interacts with one's story (that is, the outside world stops or starts cooperating, especially with the scheme aspect of one's story); second, by learning to distinguish between mood and emotion; and third, by learning to trace emotions along the emotion cycle. We'll explore the first two of these responses in the next chapter; we'll save the third one for chapter 4.

CHAPTER 3

Maddening Givens and Controlling Moods

The realities of life and the moods they induce
hinder healthy self-expression.

arah is talking with a friend in the hallway of her apartment
building. In the middle of the conversation, a fly lands on her
shoulder. She loathes flies, so she hitches up her shoulder,
hoping to dislodge the pest. No luck. After more shoulder gyra-
tions, she asks her friend to shoo the fly off. Why doesn't Sarah
just flick at the fly with her own hand? Sarah's in a wheelchair,
and one of her limits is that she cannot raise either of her hands
above the level of her chest. She can't flick flies away. Sarah is
dealing with one of the "givens" of her life.

Some things are just part of the package that comes with living
on earth. For example, it's a given that NBA centers are tall, that
government is bureaucratic, and that death will come to every
person. Some givens are common to all of us (the one about
death, for example). On the other hand, we all have givens that
are unique to us or shared by only a few (Sarah's immobility, for
instance). Either way, we can't change such givens.

No one escapes the givenness of life. Everyone has to contend
with unyielding realities. Life has a stubborn shape, and there are
parts of it we simply can't hammer into the pattern we want.

This uncooperative reality means we can't always pull off the schemes we've put in motion to make life work *our* way. For example, no matter how creatively Sarah schemes to hold her grandchildren unassisted, she'll remain physically barred from that joy. Life doesn't consult us. It simply keeps on happening. Some of it we can change; some we can't.

The notion that we can't depend on life's cooperation with our dreams and schemes is a harsh one. We naturally don't like facing it. The main way we avoid it is through living repetitively, uncreatively. That is, we do the same things, think the same thoughts, pursue the same goals, say the same stock phrases, make the same relational moves. It's as though we expect that by the sheer energy of our continual efforts we'll crush life into the shape we want. We'll conquer those nasty givens of life that enrage us at our core.

We might as well try to topple a pyramid with a crowbar. Prying on life through our best efforts will not change the major given we're discussing: that life doesn't march to the drumbeat we play, no matter how loudly we pound on our drum with a stick. Being realistic about our givens, as well as the moods that arise from them, is critical to minding our emotions.

Life's Noncooperation

Is there a biblical foundation for this idea of the noncooperation of life, or am I just being pessimistic? There is, in fact, a biblical underpinning for this idea, and it's found in Genesis 3:14-19, where we read about how God cursed his beloved creation. The outcome of the curses is threefold: creation is deformed, relationships become difficult, and human initiatives slam into disheartening obstacles. While creation still retains much beauty, while relationships sometimes work toward mutual enjoyment, while human initiative is not completely fruitless, God nevertheless releases an extravagant futility into the world to dog our weary steps.

Why, oh why, would God do this? Because he is determined to limit the success of our sin. He means to make our foolishness painful so that, mired in the muck of consequence, we might turn and seek him. It's as though we're to bounce like pinballs off the bumpers created by these curses, bounce into God's arms.

But wait — it's not only sin that meets with painful results. What about the many *moral* things people do that run into maddening perplexities? What, for example, of the couple who want to have a baby, only to end up exhausted, broke, and childless after years of fertility treatments? Heartbreakers like this serve as signs pointing out the inherent brokenness of a fallen world.

There are signs everywhere that this world doesn't suit us well and that it consequently is not our true home. We need these signs because of our pigheaded propensity to dream that we can shoehorn life into the Edenlike, homelike form we need. God sets these tragic signs in our lives to shout to us, "How could you possibly believe you could be at home here? Don't make the mistake of settling for this! If you settle for it, you'll receive so dreadfully much less than I want for you."

The heartbreaking signs call out: "Can you imagine a condition like infertility in heaven? Can you imagine cancer in your real home? How about children on drugs? Sexual abuse? Domestic violence? An arms race? Nuclear war? Environmental devastation? Shantytowns? AIDS? Lovelessness and loneliness? The collapse of the World Trade Center towers? Hitler's extermination of six million Jews?" Of course not. We'll know we're home when these predators of the soul are banished.

For now, we live in a broken world, a world where we're not at home. We ache for wholeness. We ache for home. Earth's givens — the noncooperation of life — remind us that we are surely homesick. The world is a crooked stick, a frozen bolt, a barren field, a miscarriage, a shade of gray. It's never quite right.

Collateral Damage

Someone will say, "It's not so bad, Steve. Who cut the string on your helium balloon? Lighten up, fella." Let's think about this. Is my description of the world too dismal? Well, aside from the fact that our newspapers bulge with bad news, there's the issue of how people get in a position to say, "Life's OK." My question for them is, "How many wounds have you inflicted in your journey toward making your life OK?" I'm not assuming that well-being always involves wounding others; I'm only observing that, often enough, humans will cheerfully sacrifice each other.

Take as an example the man who is regarded in his small town as a respected community pillar. He runs his own business, spreads money around, finances an annual town picnic. Great guy. Life's OK for him. But his is a deceptive façade. His second wife doesn't know it, but his first wife still has pain in her jaw where he hit her. Both his kids are deeply damaged by his cruelty and sneering lovelessness. They are two empty hearts connecting with just about any poseur who leers, "You're looking good, honey." Anything for a shred of a semblance of love.

The question is not whether life is agreeable for some but what methods are used in making it so. If the happy people are giving rise to a Third World of emotional have-nots, their smiles are hideous. Have we made sure that we have title to the fields we're harvesting? And even if so, are we leaving anything for the poor to glean? Did the small-town businessman not harvest from his children's souls a good reputation, the hypocrisy of which bears hard upon them to this day? Yes, he ignored and abused three givens — his wife and children — to steal a selfish respite from a hard world. Life would not cooperate to give him his own personal Eden, so he battered on life to yield what he demanded, and left three carcasses behind him.

That man is not fictional (though I've fictionalized key details of his life). His daughter was a counselee of mine. I asked her, "Day to day, what was he like?"

Her reply: "He was almost always angry. Even if he weren't obviously enraged, he gave off a vibe of steady irritability." From this peevishness, he could explode in an eye blink.

Such is the person who is willing to stuff others in the trash can if that's what it takes to win a little cooperation from life for his selfish plans. In his sort of unjust program, the noncooperation of life is not overcome; it is just shifted from one person to others.

And in the process, what happens in the soul of the apparently happy person is not to be happily contemplated.

Moods and Emotions

Let's gather some thoughts, draw a few conclusions based on the issues we've already considered in this chapter: First, we should regard the givens of life as a sailor would regard coral reefs in his course. He can't ignore them; he must accept that they're there and deal with them. Likewise, we must deal with the world as it actually comes to us. Further, if we try to ignore life's givens, pretending we're exempt from them, we're going to hurt others. Discounting those givens interferes with our loving our neighbor. Finally, as in the illustration of the small-town charlatan we just examined, trying to ignore the givens of life intensifies our frustration. In our anger, we end up in a limited, repetitive emotion that becomes harmful to ourselves and others.

When we're confined in same-old, same-old responses to life, the conclusion is simple: we haven't dealt with the real world effectively. We have retreated into a chronic emotional buffer. And that's why we need to understand emotions and moods better.

Moods: Fuzzy, General Feelings

Mood is a persistent state of emotion. It can last for days, even weeks. Also, mood tends to be more unfocused than emotion and thus harder to identify. People use general terms to describe their moods: a "bad mood," a "crummy mood," a "down mood," an "out-of-sorts mood." Sometimes, a mood just seems vague. You know you're bummed out, but you can't say why. Fathoming a mood can be as hard as digging holes in the ocean.

Because moods are long-term and unfocused, they can be not only hard to fathom but also hard to change. Moods are sticky. Moods are powerful. Because of their power, others can feel them radiating from us: "Man, what's wrong with Ted today? I spoke to him in the hall, and he just froze me out." Or "I was going to speak to my daughter about her attitude toward her sister, but she was so sullen I decided to wait." How many times have you changed your behavior or words because of another's mood? Clearly, mood can impact us forcefully.

That said, it's not a long leap to imagine that people may use their moods to control others. Or others may become controlled by someone else's mood without the moody one even intending it.

First, let's look at an example of someone deliberately using her mood in a controlling way. This woman feels too weak to make direct requests of others. She does not speak up and make her needs known. But she has learned that when she withdraws and pouts, the other members of her family become anxious, tentative, solicitous. She notices that they approach her carefully and wonder what she needs. Over the years, the family has settled into a let's-make-sure-withdrawn-Mom-is-OK pattern.

Second, there's the pattern of allowing oneself to be controlled by another's mood even though the other didn't intend it. An adolescent, let's say, has developed an air of hostility and touchiness. Beneath this mood, he actually wants his parents to connect with him. But his father is preoccupied with his career and often absent. His mother reads the kid's mood as "Stay the heck away!" Consulting her own depleted emotional gas tank, she's willing to retreat.

One way or another, moods can end up being misused. Where they could be invitations, they end up being weapons. And so we must keep working at understanding our moods and what causes them.

A mood is a collection of emotions. A mood is like a crowd of people all shouting at the same time. The resulting hubbub is a dull, indistinct roar. Just as a crowd can't be understood until individual voices come forward, a mood can't be understood until the focused emotions beneath it emerge.

Emotions: Feelings with a Focus

If moods are vague and hazy, emotions are clearer, more precise, more connected to a subject. It's hard to discern what moods are about, but emotions are definitely about something. For example, a woman who has been irritable for the past week (moody) is finally able to express an emotion: "I feel furious and hurt that, once again, the only reason my husband touches me is to have sex." You can probably tell a difference in your own reactions to this woman. When you read she'd been irritable for a week, you probably remembered briefly your own or others' times of irritability, and perhaps you felt mild empathy, anxiety, or annoyance. But when you read her words, you probably had a stronger reaction, perhaps strong empathy, anxiety, or anger.

Why the difference? Because mood is less focused than emotion, it doesn't demand a specific response. Do an imagination experiment: think about a woman who lives in a mildly depressed mood. Those around her may ignore her or be mildly concerned, but no one is likely to feel strongly or take decisive action toward her. Now imagine that she focuses her depressive mood and expresses emotion this way: "I'm enraged that, for thirty years, my husband has turned our children into his own personal fan club and has ignored me completely. I'm sick of being invisible." Those around her are now moved much more strongly to respond than when she was simply moody.

Emotions can be scary. They call for action. Moods are safer and are often used both to conceal emotions (because the emotions are too scary) and to gain a sense of power that compensates for the losses or frustrations underlying those unexpressed emotions. Again, think of the woman in a depressed mood versus the same woman after her open statement of emotion, of being made by her husband to feel invisible. In the latter situation, she has lost the power of subtly stimulating others to adjust to her mood. Her heart is no longer cloaked in indirect expression; it's now naked, out in the open, vulnerable. She has gained the power of honesty and lost that of stealth. Exposing one's heart is so scary that many of us prefer staying in our moods with their stealthy power.

Chronic moods, then, are often grabs for power by a person who has not learned other, more effective modes of self expression.

These unexamined moods are ineffective attempts to defeat the unpleasant givens of life we discussed earlier. As such, moods are dangers to the heart, shrink-wrap for the soul, making it small, predictable, controlling, unsurprisable, unteachable. Chronic moods program us to dance the same unreflective dance. Chronic moods are entrapments: they pull our relationships toward sameness, rarely letting us take the risks that could break old chains. Emotions, though, get us somewhere if we'll understand them and express them effectively.

Unhealthy Self-Expression

One major difference between mood and emotion, as we've already seen, is that moods are vague whereas emotions are more focused. Another major difference could be put this way: emotions are looking for words; moods are not. Let's look into this further.

Emotions are looking for words in that they are focused, they have a subject, and they can be expressed. Moods, because they're intended to stay unfocused and indirect, have little affinity for words. In fact, moods retain their power only if they're *not* transformed by words.

Because God is a self-revealing God, we who are made in his image are intended to reveal ourselves. And since God reveals himself constructively (in creation and redemption), we are meant to reveal ourselves constructively. Destructive speech is a symptom, not of healthy freedom, but of humanity's departure from God into a nasty autonomy. Humans are meant to be dependent, liberated creatures, grounded in God and thus set free to speak beneficially into the world (Ephesians 4:29).

Emotions are our signal that something inside us needs to find expression. But how do we avoid the unhealthy mania for self-expression that has torn apart so many lives and relationships? Time for a brief history lesson.

This sirocco of self-expression began in the Romantic movement that swept the Western world beginning in the late 1700s. For our purposes, all that need be said is that Romanticism doesn't trust reason and sees salvation in a return to nature. To Romantics, nature is a "great current of sympathy, running through all things," which "tells us of the importance of our own natural fulfillment and of our solidarity with our fellow creatures."[1] This notion places an enormous, unbalanced value on looking within ourselves to find what "nature" is telling us in our hearts. From this arises an emphasis on expressing ourselves and an assumption that such expression will be good in and of itself. What is inside you may differ from what is inside me, but we both have an equal right to feel and express our respective inner realities. And each is to be seen as equally valid. Your truth is true for you; mine, for me. The important thing is that we both express what's inside, trusting that our internal message, our heart's deepest longings, will turn out to be a valid, uncorrupted addition to the human spirit.

It's easy to see that this thoroughly modern idea of the automatic goodness of self-expression saturates our educational system, our art, our literature, even our science. Today, for example, I heard on the radio a serious discussion of the human heart (the actual organ) as a "neuronal structure" and therefore as a source of emotions independent of the mind. This aspect of the heart was portrayed as a trustworthy source of sentiment that takes us away from the cold, unfeeling brain, humanizes us, and makes us good. The commentators spoke as though Hallmark had implanted a sentiment-generating computer chip in every human heart (and — who knows? — perhaps in the hearts of our animal friends, too). This is the stance from which we get dreadful statements like "I had the affair because it felt right to me."

Most of us, in other words, make choices by consulting our feelings. My years in counseling confirm this. Many of my counselees have offered as the basis for their choices some variant of "I felt like it." God's Word usually comes in the loser when someone consults his feelings, especially when those feelings are intense. For example, a man who feels sexually rejected by his wife, who suffers real pain over it, often ends up consulting only his feelings when a young woman at work throws herself in his path. He may shift briefly toward God's Word if he's a Christian, but often (tragically, very often) he'll react to God's call for obedience by insisting that his intense feelings simply won't permit his answering the divine call. He comes to the fork in the road and presents his feelings as the validation for his disobedience.

This is the fruit of a culture that overemphasizes self-expression, a culture wallowing in destructive choices that devastate others and push them, in turn, to consult *their* feelings ("I'm even *more* justified in what I choose, because I'm so thoroughly victimized by my father, mother, husband, wife, whatever"). So one generation's choices breed fear and pain in the next, whose feelings intensify to an even higher pitch than the previous generation's. A vicious cycle is set in motion. An emotional prison becomes more inescapable with each generation.

I repeat, then, how can we make the healthy move from vague mood to focused emotion without embracing the unhealthy obsession with self-expression that wrecks hearts and relationships? Unless we can answer this question effectively, it would be better to return to unexpressed moods or mere numbness than to consult our emotions. We need a constructive path to follow or else our emotions will degenerate into mere appetites, swallowing our humanity and our spirituality. The upcoming chapter will develop that path.

CHAPTER 4

The Path to Greatness of Heart

Honoring our emotions enables us to learn about ourselves.

We've already seen one problem with overemphasizing our feelings—trusting our feelings without examining them ("I just felt like it") reduces each person to a self-law, immune from outside influence. "I just felt like it" is galloping selfishness—it exalts the sovereign self. "I just felt like it" simply means "I'm God." When we're in this mode, our feelings become the tablets of our law, and we tyrannize others with them even as they tyrannize us with theirs. Life turns into a war of mutual antipathies.

But we haven't seen it all yet when it comes to using our emotions as a false moral base. When overemphasized, emotions not only become a slippery slope toward selfishness; they also fool us into focusing on them to the exclusion of a much bigger picture. Emotions can be so intense that they blot out everything else inside us. Loyalty to our feelings destroys all other loyalties.

It's for this reason that we must arm ourselves to overthrow the tyranny of our feelings. It's for this reason that we must trace the connections among *all* the pieces that go together to create our emotions and our moods.

The Tyranny of Feelings

Recently I saw an example of how emotions can blot out everything else inside a person. I was in my counseling office, sitting across from someone who, for good reason, felt intense pain. Her husband had been lost in a depression for years, hadn't functioned except at work, and had rejected her sexually. "I don't feel like a woman anymore," she said. "I have this great anxiety that I'm just an empty shell and no one will ever want me again." Despite my attempts to broaden her picture by inviting her to think in scriptural categories, she kept snapping back like a rubber band to her immensely painful feelings.

Sometimes feelings can be like a hand in front of your face blocking your view of the sky. And it doesn't help that our rights to our feelings have been pitched to us through every possible venue all our waking lives. Constant, bright sloganeering about the primacy of feelings — from "If it feels good, do it" to "Where do you want to go today?" to "For everything else, there's MasterCard" — makes you feel like a misfit if you consult something other than your feelings for your motivation. But feelings should not be motivators, at least not immediately. At first, feelings should lead not to motivation but to learning. How can this happen?

We need to resist our culture's urgings to let our emotions shrink-wrap and package us as mere consumers of whatever will elevate our mood. "There's more, far more, to me than my feelings, no matter how loudly they're screaming" — this should be our response to the tyranny of feelings. On the other hand, we should not be tempted by the intense power of emotions to retreat from them, either into a too cerebral, arid response to life (all head and no heart) or into the dullness of mood-driven living (avoiding getting specific about what we feel).

So we move away from being driven by emotions, not toward arid intellectualism, not toward the vagaries of mere mood — but toward what? We need a path to walk, a way to use our emotions as fuel. The journey toward learning, especially learning about ourselves, is hard. We need energy for the journey, and this energy comes from the intensity of our emotions. It's good that our emotions are intense; otherwise, we'd never have the oomph we need to learn about ourselves. And we either learn or else we destroy.

The Emotion Cycle

If we're going to use emotions as boosters for learning, we'll need direction. The speediest rocket pointed in the wrong direction is still a disaster. Which way do we go? For starters, let's look at the emotion cycle again. It will provide us with a map to follow.

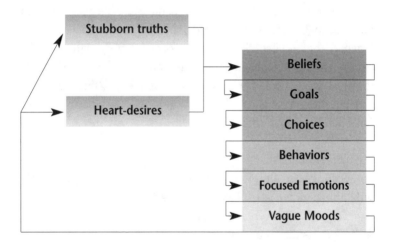

The emotion cycle above is meant to give you a map for navigating from vague moods all the way back to beliefs (what we actually believe, which is often different than what we *say* we believe). Even farther back, the emotion cycle helps you look at the stubborn truths in response to which you've formed those deepest beliefs. And the cycle leads you to explore your heart-desires, especially as they interact with the stubborn truths both of a fallen world and of God's incoming kingdom. You can start anywhere on the cycle, but it's usually easier to begin with "vague moods." That's because it's fairly easy to discern our dominant mood(s) as we move through life.

The cycle is drawn here with the arrows pointing in one direction. That's to make the important point that mood and emotions don't just happen — they have an origin, a starting place in that interplay between stubborn truths and heart-desires along with the deeply held beliefs we've formed in response to that interplay.

On the other hand, the cycle could just as well be drawn with the arrows pointing in both directions. This way of looking at the cycle emphasizes that every part of the cycle influences every other in both directions. For example, unreachable goals can reinforce deep beliefs so that someone might say, "Since I never reached that goal of having the normal family with a loving spouse along with the kids, the house, and the white picket fence, that just proves what I've always believed — that I'm a nobody." The emotion cycle is a self-education tool. Ready to go to class? Let's define some terms.

Stubborn Truths

Some things are simply true, like it or not. For example, gravity pulls things downward. Here are some more:

▶ There's a heaven and a hell.
▶ Outer space is a vacuum.
▶ God is love.
▶ Life will have hardship.
▶ Life will have joy.
▶ Laughter does you good.
▶ Male cardinals are red.
▶ Matter and energy are conserved.
▶ You can't always be first in line.
▶ Baseball is a sport; ballet is an art.
▶ Jesus is Lord.
▶ Death is inevitable.
▶ Every yes involves a no.

You can see from this list that some truths are revealed by God and some are discovered by us humans. Either way, they're true despite any wishing we might do to the contrary. And the way they collide with our desires registers powerfully on our emotions.

Heart-Desires

I get up to teach a class of high school kids. I hold forth eloquently about Genesis 3 and Adam and Eve's scrambling to avoid each other and God. The kids look at me, sphinxlike — mystery abounds in their expressions. My heart sinks. I try to start a discussion, asking, "What do you wish Adam and Eve had done instead of hiding and blaming?"

I sense an outflow of dread from the kids as if I'd proposed to show them my hernia scar. They're thinking, Uh-oh, what's the teacher looking for here?

So I say, "Don't worry about what I might want to hear. Just let your minds run on this one."

The dread goes up a notch: Now I've got to think creatively in front of my friends. Finally someone raises a hand.

Saved! I think ecstatically, calling on the blessed teen.

"Uh, like, Adam could've maybe. . . . "

In the pause a smart aleck on my right fills in with ". . . grabbed his video game controls and zapped the serpent with his vapormatic auto-laser."

I look around for a button that will open a trapdoor under this guy's chair. Or under mine.

On the way home I feel discouraged. Then I remember that another teacher had been able to get a good discussion going the previous week. I sag still more. A voice in my head says, *Who are you kidding? You teach high schoolers? Forget it. They need a real teacher.* I feel surprisingly powerful despair. What's happening here? My deep heart-desire for respect, for making a significant contribution, has collided with the stubborn truth that I can't always control my world.

The fact that I'm nearly choked with shame on the way home reveals the passion with which we yearn for two elements that are oxygen for our souls:

1. We want to *contribute,* to make a difference that is real, lasting, and bigger than we are.

2. We want to *connect,* to love and be loved without conditions, hesitations, or inhibitions.

A grand contribution. Unfettered connection. Desire for these things is what makes us human. These are the two lights of our true home.

These two longings are rooted in the image of God we bear in ourselves. Only an image-bearer can want more, can be passionate for love and impact. Only an image-bearer can thirst for more life and vitality than he has right now. In addition, only an image-bearer can shut down his heart and refuse to hope for more. Only an image-bearer can go against and hate his own longings. Only an image-bearer can sin. Only an image-bearer can lose heart. And only an image-bearer can, with God's help, reclaim his heart.

Beliefs

When I think of beliefs, I think of conflict. At first, beliefs look simple. Beliefs are simply what I affirm as true, right? Yet we need only look at my story about teaching high schoolers to see that beliefs aren't so simple. For example, someone hearing that story might say, "Steve, calm down. So you didn't get the kids in a lather about Genesis 3. It's no big deal, especially when you remember what you really believe, that God cares for you no matter what." And I really do believe that. But why isn't that belief lifting me above the shame? There must be a deeper, competing reality pressing up from within me.

In fact, there is. While I believe in God's unconditional love for me, I also vaguely but strongly believe that I'm a phony and that someday, to my great shame, I'll be exposed. The day of my exposure, I believe in some deep place, will be an unbearable nightmare, drowning me in humiliation and contempt. Some days, this counterbelief is a million miles away; some days, it's in my face like a pit bull in full attack. Why would such a belief haunt me or anyone? (Many have told me of just such beliefs that bind their souls as completely as Gulliver was bound to the earth.) To get at this, we have to go back to stubborn truths for a bit. One stubborn truth that applies here is that my deep heart-desires to contribute and to connect are like a two-sided coin. On the one side, they humanize me and call me homeward; on the other, they open me up to disappointment and heartache. They make me vulnerable because their dwelling in my heart means that what happens in my life matters desperately. My longings for contributing and connecting make me care, and because I care, I'll have real joy and sorrow. I'll be tossed about by life, and in the tossing and turmoil, I'll be impacted and formed. I'll also be deformed. We could say that at the beginning of our lives God forms us; then life further forms and deforms us; finally, through Christ and his Spirit, God reforms us. None of this would be possible if we were not image-bearers whose hearts long to contribute and connect. The fact that we're made for heaven also makes us vulnerable to counterfeits of heaven. This conflict is there from the moment we're born.

As we grow up, we're tossed about by events and relationships that deeply impress us, causing us to learn. We draw conclusions, try them out, keep the ones that seem to work (whether they're founded on truth or not), and throw away those that don't. The more insulated we are from feedback and godly modeling, the more faulty our learning may be. Add the concept that our minds are darkened by sin (Ephesians 4:17-18), and it's easy to see how error-ridden our beliefs might become. And since these beliefs had (and still have) survival value, they cling to us like barnacles to a piling.

In fact, life's pain steers us to believe that whatever moves us from pain to safety is good, is beyond criticism. Without feedback from outside, we foolishly cherish any behavior, attitude, emotion, or thought pattern that transports us out of pain and toward safety. The more we figure out what works to reduce the ache and increase the comfort, the less we *want* outside feedback — it might shift us out of our comfort zone, cut our lifeline. We end up self-sufficient, sealed off from feedback. We monitor others, not to get input, but to see whether our painstakingly constructed defenses are working. Nothing that works to help our safety campaign must be disturbed. So, while I believe that God loves me no matter what, I also have a foolish belief that I have to earn approval constantly so that I'm not seen as incompetent.

Again, when I think of beliefs, I think of conflict. We can now see that the conflict is rooted in a deep split within our hearts, a split the Bible conceives as a rivalry between the "old man" and the "new man." Coming to Christ in faith and being thus born again does not wipe out the old man, even though it does deal him a severe blow. The Christian life is, among other things, a life of conflict between the beliefs of the new creature in Christ and these stubborn, survival-driven beliefs of the old man.

Goals

The goals in the emotion cycle are not the conscious ones of normal goal setting (as in "My goal is to get caught up at the office by the end of the week"). Instead, they are goals lodged deeply in our hearts, goals we often overlook and even deny having. For example, the high school kid who interrupted with the wisecrack may have had the goal of drawing attention to himself or of impressing others with his quick mind. But he didn't think that in the split second before he interrupted. His goal has been second nature for so long that it drives his behavior without his thinking about it.

Everything we do, then, may be traced to a covert yet intentional collection of goals that are, in turn, based on what we believe (not just what we say we believe). So our behavior will always make sense to anyone who pursues the deep intentions of our hearts.

Consider this example: An adolescent refuses to use the hall bathroom, insisting instead on using his parents' bathroom. The parents feel they have no privacy, and they want their bathroom back. Others advise them to get tough with the child, establish firm boundaries, and so on. Not bad advice, perhaps, but the situation doesn't improve until the parents finally think to ask their son, "What's your intention in avoiding the hall bathroom?" After some probing, he reveals that he hates the hall bathroom because, at ages six and seven, he was physically abused there by his father several times. The son's goal is to avoid a painful place (and maybe also to punish his father in a subtle way for the abuse). Once his goals are unearthed, his behavior makes sense. Now the parents, while sticking to their original plan (they still want their bathroom back), can also seek to restore their broken relationship with their son.

The fact that every life is a collection of goals means that each life is on the move, heading in a definite direction. All of us are journeying.

My friend Sarah, who (as I mentioned in the previous chapter) can't lift her arm to shoo a fly away, sits in a wheelchair all day within the confines of a nursing home. Sarah is doubly restrained: limited to a movable chair, limited to the square footage of the nursing home. Yet Sarah journeys far each day. Her journey involves fighting off the indignities of her limitations and maintaining her self-respect. This she must accomplish anew each day.

One day I asked Sarah, "What's it like to be in that wheelchair day after day?"

She addressed me with utter earnestness: "I think of this wheelchair as God's gift. He has me here to make me more like Jesus."

In Sarah's case, the journey is from indignity to self-respect. She accomplishes her journey by drawing daily on the liberating, encouraging words of Jesus to her heart.

To expand her story so that it captures all of our journeys, we could say that every one of us struggles to journey away from pain and toward safety. The givens of life collide with us from the day we're born, sometimes interfering with our journey. George Herbert, the Christian poet, put it this way: "I was born crying, and every day shows why."[1] These things we can't change strike hard at our need to believe we can preserve our own emotional well-being.

If we were sinless, we'd say, "I'm afraid and hurt. Now I'll go to my Father and pour out my heart until he restores my soul." Because we're not sinless, we're prone to say, "I'm in desperate pain, but I cannot and must not trust God for healing. He'll just let me down like everyone else. I've got to dig out of this on my own." Thus begins the journey of self-sufficiency. Based on what we believe will get us out of pain, we set goals that direct our journey toward *our* version of safety.

Choices

People's goals predispose them to certain choices. For example, one whose goal is to be unobtrusive probably will not choose to run for student body president. A man whose goal is to be the "tough guy" will likely choose not to attend "chick flicks" with his wife. The important point here is that these are choices, not outcomes that are fated ahead of time. We often arrive at forks in the road, but we're so used to choosing our familiar boundaries that we miss the truth that we have real freedom, real choices.

Behaviors

People's goals and choices (inner realities) result in certain behaviors (outward actions). We don't emit random behaviors; rather, our behavior is the flowering of whatever motives reside deep within us. If you want to know what someone desires, watch how she behaves.

Whenever I visit my friend Sarah, I never fail to find that she has, with the help of her caregivers, pinned two or three jewelry butterflies onto her sweatshirt or blouse. These brooches signify her desire to be free and her belief that, with Christ, she'll be truly free one day. Some of her caregivers grumble about having to pin the butterflies on her each morning. They've missed the fact that her behavior (asking them to pin butterflies on her) signifies her desire for freedom. Again, if you want to know what someone desires, watch her behavior.

Focused Emotions

Every day, we launch our canoe into a brand-new flow of the people-and-events stream. That stream never stopped moving as we slept, and it presents us with different conditions than the ones we knew when we went to bed. As we wake, it floods onward, full tilt. It doesn't consult us as we stumble out of bed. It never, for example, asks me, "Steve, are you up to this today? Would you rather I slowed down for you or took the exact course you'd like for today? Maybe you'd like a day where you get paid double for not going to work? Or a day where your middle-aged body feels like it's twenty again? Or you have all the hair back on your head? Or a day where people drop by every hour to tell you how much they love you? Or a week where chocolate cake has neither calories nor fat? Gee, Steve, just tell me; you can program life to be whatever you want." I know, I know, I'm laughing out loud, too. This ain't heaven, is it?

Decidedly not. Instead, the people-and-events stream, heedless of our own small journey from pain to safety, roars around us. We journey in a hurricane. On top of that, we're trying to do something rather delicate — find life for our sometimes frail, uncertain hearts. So, what life amounts to is doing heart surgery in a hurricane. Our focused emotions reflect how we're doing at this impossible task.

If our self-guided tour from pain to safety is going well, our emotions will generally be up. If not, they'll be down. But as we saw in chapter 3, our up or down emotions can mislead us.

When a comedian has the audience roaring with laughter, he'll feel good. He may conclude that he has arrived at maximum safety, that his journey from pain to safety is effective and commendable. But this is not at all what God meant for his emotions to teach him. Rather, he should learn from his up emotions something like this: *My glad heart is telling me two things: first, that something in me loves to be honored, and second, that I've concluded that stimulating others into liking me is the way to get honor.* The first insight — that the comedian loves to be honored — stems from his deep longings to connect and to contribute. The second insight — that he stimulates others to emit the approval he wants — stems from his false belief that he alone must control the sources of his well-being. This belief is essentially a conviction that he lives in a closed universe, that there's no one out there with a plan for him or with supplies to sustain him within that plan.

Someone will say, "Wait! That may be true for an unbeliever, but I'm a Christian. I believe we live in an *open* universe. God is there for me, and I am resting in him."

No doubt this is true for many of us, but our behavior often reveals that our belief in a universe opened by a God of love exists in furious competition with counterbeliefs that reflect a closed universe in which survival is up to us. As we saw in our discussion on beliefs, this inner war shouldn't surprise us. The Bible assures us that "the flesh wages war against the spirit and the spirit against the flesh" (Galatians 5:17, my paraphrase). The point of learning from our focused emotions is not to see whether our pain-to-safety strategies are working but to see whether they are godly. It's important to learn from our emotions, because they will tell us whether we believe the universe is closed or open. Our emotions, if we'll learn from them, will tell us whether we're functional atheists or functioning believers. (Of course, a God of grace can handle our times of functional atheism and love us out of them.)

In chapter 2 we discussed the idea of story. We talked about themes, dreams, and schemes, about how they weave together to form the story in which we're living, whether we acknowledge it or not. Now we can take the idea of story a bit further by saying that learning from our emotions reveals the extent to which our stories are compatible with God's. We've already seen that our up or down emotions can't be counted on to tell us anything immediately. In fact, as we've seen, they may mislead us into thinking we're in a good story or a bad story, when reality may be quite different. What I'm urging here is that we learn from our emotions rather than jumping to conclusions based on what we feel, no matter how strong those feelings are.

Vague Moods

As soon as the last paragraph ends by discussing "what we feel," we're challenged to maintain our division between focused emotions and vague moods. As we've seen, just because we feel something doesn't mean there's any focus to it. Some people live their entire lives in a vague, unexamined mood.

One man I know (let's call him Joseph) has been running scared from the downdrag of depression since his early teens. He wouldn't call it a depressive feeling; in fact, he is so busy running from it that he doesn't know what to call it. Joseph only knows that he wants himself far away from it. He evades it through a never-ending devotion to his work. He hates weekends because, undistracted by work, he feels the cloud of depression moving in.

This vague mood so scares Joseph that he lives in a story whose main theme is fear of depression, whose main dream is a depression-free world, and whose main scheme is escaping depression through work. His up emotions tell him that he has successfully escaped through work; his down emotions tell him that he is sliding toward failure (the depression will "get" him) and he'd better enlarge his escape-through-work strategy.

No, no, no! Joseph has drawn the wrong conclusions. His conclusions are deadly to every covenant in his life; no relationship (no matter how strong his marriage vow or his promises to his kids) is safe from the encroachment of his work. A terrified man cannot love well. A man pursued by the demon of depression will run over everyone who needs him to slow down.

So, what is the *right* conclusion? What should Joseph learn? First, he should move from vague mood to focused emotion. His mood is tense, frustrated, all the time screaming, "Leave me alone!" It is the mood of a man who is running. To move toward focused emotion, he needs to stop running and turn and face the depression. What has been chasing him all those years? Until he answers this, it will be worse than useless to give him instruction in managing his work better ("three steps to effective time management" or some such approach). He doesn't *want* to manage his work better. The *point* is to generate more work, to stay inefficient. Only by facing the depression and entering his focused emotions will he be able to learn about the story in which he is caught.

Second, Joseph needs to use his depression as fuel to move him along the rest of the emotion cycle. But that's a bigger subject, one that we'll tackle in the next chapter. There we'll use what we know of him to illustrate how we can put the emotion cycle to work in our own lives.

CHAPTER 5

Longings Versus Realities

When what we want collides with what is true,
we are invited to grow.

In the last chapter we met a man named Joseph who uses work to run from depression. His overcommitment to his job strains every important relationship in his life. Can this situation change? Or are the people who love him doomed to getting only leftovers from him? The leverage for change (and he *can* change) will come when this man deals with the collision that has occurred between stubborn truths and his heart-desires.

The same is true for another man, Daniel, whom we will meet after we're through with Joseph. Daniel's life shows the pain that can be caused when longings butt up against the harsh realities of the world. But his life also shows how understanding the emotion cycle can lead to a release into the freedom God wants for us.

We all know what it's like to experience the head-on collision of what we want with what is true. The crumpled metal. The shards of glass on the pavement. But there is hope for all of us in minding our emotions.

The Abuse of Longings

As we learned in the last chapter, every person has two fundamental longings: to contribute and to connect. But we don't have to pay attention to our longings. In fact, most of us don't. (Our culture doesn't help here. It tells us that we are producers by day and consumers in our off hours — and that this is all we are.) Obeying our culture and our own foolish hearts, we both squelch and pervert our longings. We squelch them when we ignore them and hold them in contempt. We pervert them by trying to attach them to some substitute good. This usually happens in sequence: first we squelch our longings, then they resurface somewhere else in perverted form.

Now let's go back to our workaholic, Joseph. He perverts his desire to contribute by steering into a typical modern career path. He doesn't ask the question, "How might God call me to a particular station in life as I serve his kingdom?" Rather, he asks, "How can I use work to avoid my depression, make enough money to survive, and attain a teaspoonful of self-respect?" By twisting his longing to contribute, he routes himself into a smaller story than the one for which God made him. Being called by God to serve in a vital theater in a furious war on the side of God's kingdom, a war laced with victories, defeats, passionate defenses, and ringing cries — such a calling is far more fulfilling than the death-of-a-salesman, self-diminishing role that modern careerism presents us with. The world of labor has degenerated into a swirl of per-verted, shrunken longings.

Not only is Joseph shrinking his desire to *contribute;* he's also completely denied his longing to *connect.* No one, including his wife and kids, really knows him. His only style of connecting is through arguing with his wife; he knows no other intimacy. His kids see him as a mystery. They love him, but they don't get what he's about, so they shrug and mainly just do their own thing.

Joseph's Stubborn Truths

Let's switch to the category of stubborn truths. There are at least three of them in this situation. First, you can't disown longings completely. They'll reemerge somewhere else and demand satis-faction. Second, disowned and perverted longings lead to places that can't truly satisfy. Third, the pain of dissatisfaction is meant to lead us to God.

No one can alter these truths. They are fixed points. Just as an anchor keeps a ship from drifting, so a stubborn truth keeps a soul from drifting. But a ship is a dumb object; a person is not. People — made in God's image and thus given freedom — can choose to ignore stubborn truths, especially when they collide with insistent longings. Ignoring truths doesn't make them untrue; it just makes them dangerous. For example, Joseph is ignoring the truth that disowned longings will, at last, resurface and demand satisfaction. His longing for connection, denied in his marriage because of his work commitments, reemerges when his secretary starts listening to his troubles. Her sympathetic ear accentuates her desirable figure. He feels superficially good in connecting with her, but he's sliding toward a whole nest of vipers. Their bite will feel much more than superficially miserable.

Rather than shunning the stubborn truths at any juncture in our lives, it's urgent that we come to grips with them without flinching. Truth is not always sweet (as our culture tends to present it). Rather, truth can be tart, even sour. Yet swallowing it can be a discipline that "yields the peaceful fruit of righteousness" (Hebrews 12:11). We must face whatever stubborn truth affects us, which is what our emotions are telling us to do.

But when emotions are intense, we're tempted to ditch the truth and satisfy our longings. Deep longings and stubborn truths often battle. We long to connect, but if we connect indiscriminately and selfishly (like Joseph with that secretary), we'll pay a price and so will others. *Crash!* Another collision on life's highway.

To take this further, let's look at a story of tragic connections in the life of another man, whom we'll call Daniel.

Tragic Connections

Daniel came for counseling after his fourth affair. His long-suffering wife had finally given him an ultimatum: "Get help or get out!" As Daniel began to explore the insecurities beneath his sin of adultery, he disclosed the secret that, beginning when he was about ten, his older brother had beaten him and sexually abused him for several years. Daniel surfaced from the abuse with a deep fear that he might have homosexual tendencies since his brother was "attracted" to him. His primary emotion was anxiety (Am I gay?). He covered the anxiety with a low-level depression that fogged in most of his days. He avoided this down feeling through smoking and staying maniacally busy. His multiple affairs were, in part, an attempt to reassure himself that he was attractive to women (that is, unattractive to men).

Two tragic connections dominate this story: first, the one Daniel's brother cruelly created through abusing him; and second, the connection Daniel made whenever he had an affair with a woman in his attempts to scrub off the stain of abuse. Both connections were illegitimate and inexcusable, although we have more compassion for one who is trying to scour off a stain. Both connections were forged when emotions became drivers of behavior rather than bearers of a message. When Daniel became emotion-driven instead of emotion-educated, he and his wife (and others) got crunched in the collision of desire and truth. If only he had allowed his emotions to convey their true message, the collision needn't have happened.

What could the message be? The message is some variation on this theme: desire, whether frustrated or fulfilled, is meant to lead us to God. As G. K. Chesterton once observed, the man who knocks on the door of a brothel is looking for God. The problem is that the man at the brothel door is taking the short cut of looking for easy satiation instead of true satisfaction. But if we listen to our emotions, we'll learn that our desires are for something far greater than quick-fix satiation.

Daniel exemplifies this. Reacting to sexual abuse by his brother, he formed a deep desire to show that he was attractive to women and was neither weak nor gay. *Do I have what it takes as a man?* Daniel wondered. His desire focused on proving that he could measure up.

But how is he going to prove himself? How will he carry out his desire to measure up as a man? Because he has been injured in his sexuality, he instinctively chooses to prove himself sexually by attracting women to himself. His emotion (anxiety) drives him toward compulsive sexual behavior. Some would call him a "sex addict" — a term that, while not inaccurate, gives an incomplete picture of the struggle going on in Daniel's heart.

OK, so he will prove himself sexually. But how many partners will be enough? Daniel doesn't know. How much can his conscience stand? He doesn't know. Again, because he's driven by his emotions rather than learning from them, he deteriorates into a brute with an aching conscience and a dying marriage.

Through the Emotion Cycle

Listening to his anxiety rather than being driven by it would lead him in quite a different direction. How would he do this? Let's go back to our emotion cycle. First of all, Daniel is not actually aware of his anxiety. More likely, he's aware of a vague mood, one that says something like this: Sometimes I just feel antsy, kind of agitated and freaked out inside. So he smokes a cigarette and gets busy around the house. Or he picks a fight with his wife.

On our cycle, though, he's invited to do something else — that is, to stop and reflect on the more focused emotion underneath the vague mood. Then he might admit: I'm anxious and fearful. Following the map further, he could — maybe for the first time — connect this emotion with his behaviors. (No wonder I'm smoking two packs a day — I stay anxious most of the time.) He might also clarify the source of other behaviors. (I don't really hate my wife; I just fight with her to keep my mind off the fear and guilt inside.)

Then the issue of choice (still following the cycle) comes to the forefront. Daniel admits that none of these behaviors is as necessary as they feel when he does them. In fact, they're a matter of choice; they're intentional. He owns up to the fact that he intends to smoke, pick fights, have affairs, and stay overly busy. At first he's surprised: why would anyone choose to do these things?

Then he's relieved: You mean I'm not a robot, and I'm not doomed to repeat this pattern all my life? I have a choice?

Intrigued, he takes the step from looking at choices to exploring goals. If he's doing these things intentionally, he must be trying to reach a goal. What might be the goal of choosing conflict, affairs, smoking, busyness, and so on? After some reflection and prayer, he realizes that his goal is to prove beyond a doubt that he's "man enough." In a counseling session, the ensuing conversation might go something like this:

COUNSELOR: Man enough to do what?

DANIEL: I'm not sure. Maybe man enough to be attractive to women.

COUNSELOR: OK, but I'm not sure that's where it stops. What else might be going on?

DANIEL: Well, I, uh, don't really like to say this, but man enough to know I don't attract men.

COUNSELOR: Why is that so important to you?

DANIEL: Because, well, you know, my brother. . . .

COUNSELOR: What about him?

DANIEL: Well, he wouldn't have done anything to me if, maybe, I'd been more . . . if I'd been stronger or something.

COUNSELOR: You think something about you is weak and that your weakness drew your brother to take advantage of you?

DANIEL: Yeah.

Now we're arriving at a very important place on our cycle. Daniel is getting close to a core belief: that if he appears soft and weak, another man will prey on him. And, somehow, that will be his fault. He'll deserve whatever abuse he gets.

What harsh beliefs! Why would anyone hang on to them? The answer is twofold: we hang on to wrong beliefs (even those that make us miserable) because of our powerful desires and our determined foolishness. To bear this out, let's continue our conversation with Daniel:

COUNSELOR: The way you think of your weakness as a young boy—it's like you think you could have helped it somehow.

DANIEL: Well, I know I was only a little boy, but something in me tells me it was my fault.

COUNSELOR: What was your fault?

DANIEL: Being weak.

COUNSELOR: What would be scary about considering that it *wasn't* your fault?

DANIEL: You mean my brother did what he did just because he wanted to, not because I drew him to it somehow?

COUNSELOR: Yes.

DANIEL: Then I'd really be unprotected. I mean, bad stuff can just happen and there's no way to account for it.

COUNSELOR: So your weakness as a boy is your way of accounting for it and explaining why it happened?

DANIEL: Yeah.

COUNSELOR: Why's it so important to explain that it happened in a way that blames *you*?

DANIEL: Then maybe I can change what made it happen by changing myself.

COUNSELOR: So, if you blame yourself, you're more in control?

DANIEL: That's right.

A strong desire is coming to light: the desire for control and for safety through control. It's a desire so strong that Daniel wrongly blames himself for his own sexual abuse. That way, he thinks, he can make himself a smaller target for violation.

While we can feel a certain amount of compassion for him, we also need to be honest enough to say, "This is foolish," for one of the stubborn truths in this situation is that the human heart is darkened and foolish (Ephesians 4:17-19). It's simply foolish to maintain a self-injuring belief in order to gain a semblance of control in a tiny corner of safety that excludes God. When strong desires mingle with determined foolishness, the heart shrinks and becomes imprisoned in a too small story. Our emotions have a message that beckons and urges us to turn from that story into God's larger tale of redemption, release, and restoration. Our emotions contain God's dynamite for the soul, his striving to blast us out of a heart-killing story into a narrative of new life. Our emotions, used as teachers, can take us from death to life. Sad to say, we seldom listen to our emotions that way; rather, we treat them as mental adrenaline, meant to generate immediate action. We hurry through our emotions. Instead, we should meditate on them, contemplating where they might lead and what they might tell us.

This takes us to the issue of desire and what we choose to do with it. Our choices about our desires determine whether we take the godly path with our emotions or let ourselves get sidetracked onto some route that leads us away from the destination God has in mind for us.

CHAPTER 6

Desires of the Heart

What we want affects how we feel—and what
we do with those feelings.

What steals us away from listening to our emotions? In a nut-
shell, the misuse of our emotions comes from the corrup-
tion of our longings. Our heart's desires will often tempt us
to let our emotions drive us rather than teach us. But this does *not*
mean that our desires, in and of themselves, are necessarily wrong.

The center of the human is desire. Humans cannot live apart
from desire. As writer John Eldredge says, "Ecstasy is not an
option."[1] Sadly, though, Christians have not always been comfortable with normal human desire. Another writer, Sam Storms,
puts it this way: "One of the worst injustices the church has per-
petrated against its members is proclaiming a message of the evil
of desire."[2] If we want to learn how to use our emotions for our
benefit, we'll have to learn how to understand and properly direct
our legitimate desires.

In this chapter we'll look at three focal points in Scripture
that give us three angles of vision regarding our desires. First,
using 1 Corinthians 1:23, we'll look at why we're sometimes afraid
of desire. Second, using James 4:1-3, we'll look at desire that's out
of control. Third, using Isaiah 55:1-3, we'll see desire as it's meant
to be: under a word from God and thus invited to be its true self.

Fear of Feeling

In 1 Corinthians 1:23 Paul said, "We preach Christ crucified, to Jews a stumbling block and to Gentiles foolishness." The word for "Gentiles" is more literally translated "Greeks." What did Paul mean when he said the gospel is foolishness to the Greeks? And what can we learn about our emotions from this argument?

For Paul, Greek learning represented the epitome of the "wisdom of men" (1 Corinthians 2:5). The ancient Greeks relied on rationality, assuming that the unaided human mind, working at its best, could piece together the answers to essential questions, both practical and ultimate. By Paul's day, the Greeks had long believed in the autonomy of reason and believed that humans, ready to grow away from dependence on gods, could establish an independence founded on the functioning of their unfettered minds.

This sort of overemphasis on rationality did not die out with the ancient Greeks. The same tendency lives on today, and it has many consequences. The consequence that concerns us at the moment is distrust of the human heart whenever it inclines toward emotion. Emotionless rationality is barren and leads to a stoic mind-set. Instead of feeling deeply and using one's mind to learn from those feelings, rational stoics tend to analyze everything from a distance, emotion-free. But life is not a jigsaw puzzle — something to be regarded dispassionately as a problem to be solved. It is (at first, anyway) a tragedy, and tragedies are meant to be felt, not analyzed.

The stoic mind-set, reducing everything to ABC basics, ends up heartless. The mind overly focused on analysis destroys the heart because it doesn't trust the heart. It holds the heart in contempt, despising anything that's "weak" enough to feel.

Picture a frustrated father driving home with his family from his son's football game. A poisonous silence hangs in the air. The son, all of thirteen and the quarterback for his team, just threw three interceptions in a loss. One of the interceptions occurred because the boy hurried a throw rather than get hit by an onrushing linebacker. His father, disgusted, has decided the boy is a "coward" (at thirteen!). When they get home, the father says, "Come into the front yard with me, boy." His mother and siblings watch in horror as the father says, "Now, tackle me." The boy tries to object, but the father screams, "Tackle me! Don't be a sissy!" The mother protests, and the father furiously orders her inside. Muttering, she complies. So the boy hurls himself at his father (who outweighs him by seventy-five pounds) over and over. Furious and helpless, the boy finally stalks into the house.

His heart wanted to cry out, "Dad! Believe in me anyway! Teach me! Show me! Encourage me! Don't reject me or humiliate me!" But he assumed that his father wouldn't hear, so he surrendered his heart to his intellect, which had told him, "Don't bother showing how you feel. It'll just make it worse. Hide your heart. Just take the punishment and learn to think ahead so you avoid these embarrassments in the future." Of course, when he thinks ahead, the boy decides initiative is a dangerous thing (after all, quarterbacking is all about taking initiatives), so he drifts away from risk taking and into passivity and detachment. The result? Another emasculated male, up in his head all the time, killing his heart over and over. Another braveheart lost to life's battle.

Do the head and the heart have to be enemies? Does intellect always kill emotion? No. Early American theologian Jonathan Edwards wrote, "Religion consists so much in affection, as that without holy affection there is no true religion: and no light in the understanding is good, which [doesn't] produce holy affection in the heart."[3] God designed us to be integrated, whole beings, with emotion, mind, imagination, will, and body working together in complete harmony. Otherwise, why would he command us to love him with all our heart, soul, mind, and strength (Deuteronomy 6:5; Mark 12:30)? Inner unity, not fragmentation, is our heritage. Wholeness is our birthright, not an internal chaos where one capacity competes with the others for domination.

Let's revisit the scenario in which the father ordered his son to tackle him. In the former scene, the boy's mind squelched his emotions, not because his mind was too strong, but because it was too weak! A strong mind would have presented these thoughts to the boy: "You're right to feel the injustice of what your father wants you to do. Tell him you understand his frustration but that you won't participate in an unjust handling of it. You'll need to be strong as you say these things, so become even *more* aware of your passion for justice. And while you're at it, check into your passion for your father, your longing for him to find the part of himself that wants to teach you instead of bully you. Don't give up on your father; believe in him just as you want him to believe in you." If you find yourself reading this and thinking, *How likely is it that a thirteen-year-old is going to say these things?* you're missing the point. The point is this: the reason kids are not likely to say such things is that they aren't taught to have a strong mind with a strong link to emotions.[4]

Surprisingly, rational stoicism ends up devaluing the mind as much as it does the heart. The mind and the heart work best in tandem, and that's what the stoic forgets. The wise thinker is one who pays attention to the desires residing deep in the heart.

Emotion in the Driver's Seat

If the stoic mind overrides the heart, does that mean we should rev up our emotions and blow past the intellect with accelerated feelings? Do we follow the dictates of pop psychology and simply vent?

By now you know the answer. Letting the pendulum swing all the way from extreme rationalism to extreme emotionalism is no improvement. Venting any emotion at any time is harmful to anyone within the radius of the effect, including the one who is venting. Researchers have learned that the indiscriminate expression of emotion actually serves to intensify that emotion, not release it. Expressing anger, for example, usually makes you more angry, not less.[5]

We live in a culture that encourages the expression of emotion on the grounds that repressed emotions somehow turn into toxins inside us. Scripture, however, comes down on the side of caution about the expression of emotion. This is a caution that doesn't slide too far, doesn't become stoic. Somewhere between stoicism and ventilationist fantasies, the Bible occupies a position on emotions we might label "careful respect." Our emotions *should* be respected, not considered weak, selfish, or sinful per se. On the other hand, they're to be handled with care and not allowed to overwhelm our hearts or the hearts of others.

The Bible's caution comes from the recognition that ungoverned feelings can push our normal desires and longings into lust. Desire is vital (numbness is the only alternative), yet we must interpret desire carefully or it will become infinite. As philosopher Paul Ricoeur puts it, unrestrained desire will degenerate into an "infinity of desire . . . a desire of desire,"[6] with the result that it will never be enough to be a finite creature. In our longing to be infinite, we seek to become as God. Since our grasp must not, we think, fall short of our reach — no matter how far we reach — we get lulled into thinking that our wishes express God's will. Worshiping our wishes and cutting ourselves off from God's comfort, we create a flaming urgency to grasp and consume. We "allege the irresistibility of our passions in order to justify ourselves" (Ricoeur again).[7]

James 4:1-3 depicts desire gone rotten. As desire decays into lust, as we justify our grasping for life on our own terms, we trample relationships in our drive for selfish satisfaction.

> What is the source of quarrels and conflicts among you? Is not the source your pleasures that wage war in your members? You lust and do not have; so you commit murder. You are envious and cannot obtain; so you fight and quarrel. You do not have because you do not ask. You ask and do not receive, because you ask with wrong motives, so that you may spend it on your pleasures.

James sees the result of the heart's becoming enslaved to feelings without the benefit of a strong intellect. Without the counterforce of thought, emotion can degenerate into moodiness, longings into lust. Any delay between wanting and having then becomes intolerable, enraging. Deprivation becomes a personal insult, the only response to which is willful, harsh possessiveness. No wonder the tenth commandment rings out, "Thou shalt not covet" (Exodus 20:17, KJV)!

When Christ is not the center of our lives, when we revoke the command not to covet, the heart becomes a stew of contending passions ("your pleasures . . . wage war in your members"). I saw this recently in marital counseling. When I asked the husband why he had had an affair, he cited the fact that his wife had shut him out emotionally. Because Christ is not the center of his life, he refused to tolerate any delay between wanting and having. Without Christ as the reference point, he had no resources for waiting and suffering in faith that his Lord would never shut him out, would welcome his prayers and pain, and would use his time of distress to deepen his character. His anger became the dominant passion of his heart, and it led him to give his heart to another woman, thus wounding his marriage. "You lust and do not have," says James; "so you commit murder." Here, a marriage was murdered.

A less obvious example is the man who moves through life deciding who are the most desirable women around him in a given setting, then fantasizing about what it would be like to sleep with each of them. He never acts out his sordid mental sexualizing, but he is an adulterer nonetheless. He lusts in an entirely private way, but he grasps women and objectifies them as effectively as though he had literally pursued them. What do we find at the bottom of this habit? For him, anger at rejections that came during high school — a socially awkward time for this man. The anger has driven him to process and possess women mentally. His other capacities (intellect, will, imagination) have not been strong enough to push his emotions out of the driver's seat. His emotion (anger) has acted on his longing (for justice) and pushed it into a lust for vengeance.

Emotions Under a Word from God

The problem with the let-it-all-hang-out, ventilationist position is that it treats emotions as autonomous, as free from critique, as deserving of unqualified respect and freedom. This position flies in the face of the Scriptures' basic presupposition, which is that every created thing (and every aspect of things created, such as emotion) is to come under a word from God, who discerns all things and speaks to all things the truth that brings them to peace. So our emotions should speak, but they should also be spoken to — that is, they should receive the word God would say to them.

Isaiah 55:1-3 permits us to let our hearts speak and yet also encourages our hearts to hear from God:

> Ho! Every one who thirsts, come to the waters;
> And you who have no money come, buy and eat.
> Come, buy wine and milk
> Without money and without cost.
> Why do you spend money for what is not bread,
> And your wages for what does not satisfy?
> Listen carefully to Me, and eat what is good,
> And delight yourself in abundance.
> Incline your ear and come to Me.
> Listen, that you may live.

"Listen!" this passage insists, as if to say, "Someone is calling to you with a message so important that it must interrupt everything!" What is this interrupting message? What is so urgent that we must turn from our plans and priorities to hear it?

The interrupting message starts by addressing "everyone who thirsts." This phrase carries two blessings: First, it is universal, calling out to *everyone* who thirsts. Second, the call *assumes* thirst. It doesn't address "everyone who thinks or wills or imagines or behaves in such and such a way." No, it addresses *thirst*. As important as these other capacities are, thirst is deeper still. Thirst speaks of the heart's basic condition, that of lacking and desiring.

Why is thirst more basic even than thinking, willing, imagining, or acting? Because our thinking, willing, imagining, and acting are *about* thirst. On our emotion cycle chart (chapter 4), thirst is described in the phrase *heart-desires,* which comes *before* beliefs, goals, and the others. We think, believe, choose, and so forth because we're driven by the itch of longing. How shall we scratch this itch? This is the question that leads us to think and choose. Depending on the success or failure of our various ways of answering that question, our emotions come to life. If we scratch the itch of longing successfully, we feel good; if not, we feel bad.

But as we've already seen, these feelings need to be interpreted, not just taken as votes confirming or denying our ways of scratching the itch of longing. We interpret them by tracing them through the emotion cycle. Otherwise, we're in danger of assuming that whatever makes us feel good is good and whatever makes us feel bad is bad.

Isaiah 55 never comes close to imagining that things can be labeled "good" simply because they make us feel good. That would result in a tyranny of hedonism under which Isaiah 55 would read, "Everyone who thirsts, come to whatever reliably makes you feel good." Rather, Isaiah 55 embraces all who thirst with the invitation "Come to the waters." In other words, "Bring all of your longings and their accompanying emotions to a source of refreshment and life."

The call to "come" cuts across our anxious, shortsighted drama on the stage of life. We're invited away from writing our own lines, directing our own play. We're invited to consider lines from a script far greater than our own. We're invited to relax into a theme that takes us out of the exhausting center of things.

Surely such an invitation comes only to the privileged and powerful. The silky, sultry celebrities must be the intended audience, right? But no, for Isaiah 55 goes on to say, "You who have no money come, buy and eat." The invitation reaches out for the poor, the tired, the dispossessed, the humble, the disqualified. In fact, the rich and powerful are in danger of spending their resources foolishly: "Why do you spend . . . your wages for what does not satisfy?" Implication: nothing so trivial as a purchase can truly satisfy us, no matter how much money is involved. No consumer item or real property can bring true peace and wholeness. No tangible possession can scratch the itch of longing.

These are heretical words in the Western world, I know. Are we moderns and postmoderns not rigorously trained to have faith in the marketplace? Are we not disciplined severely to bow down to Mammon? Yet Isaiah 55 dares to say, "It's a hoax! You cannot consume your way to peace. The empty soul cannot fill itself, no matter how great its resources." So Isaiah 55 invites the thirsty heart away from the grotesque golden cow of the marketplace and toward — what? A plan? A prophecy? A power? In some ways, all three of these are included, but all are valid only as they are wrapped up in a *Person*.

After the invitation to the thirsty, Isaiah moves on to say,

> Listen carefully to *Me,* and eat what is good,
> And delight yourself in abundance.
> Incline your ear and come to *Me.*
> Listen, that you may live. (emphasis added)

Now we're told of the only water that will quench our thirst, the only bread that will assuage our hunger. We're told quite emphatically that only a Person can satisfy us, and only as we are intimate with that Person can we truly live. We find that *listening* to this One is the key to satisfied desire.

What is listening? It consists of coming under the full influence of a word from outside ourselves. Isaiah 55 says we are to "incline our ears." That is, we're to lean toward the speaking mouth of God, as it were, lean in so as to catch the merest whisper of what he might say to us. The idea is that even his softest murmurs carry delicacies for our hungry hearts. Real satisfaction depends on a word from outside us, one we can't supply for ourselves. Listening is a sign of dependency and need, a sign that we are not the masters of our lives. Listening is a sign that we are made for God.

If we're to listen to God, why listen to our emotions? Because our emotions can lead us back to our thirst for God when our hearts have drifted away from him. Listening to our emotions convinces us that we need to listen to God.

Today I ran into a buzz saw of a woman in counseling. Her words emerged from a cold, hard heart. I felt as if I were approaching an iceberg with an ice pick. The session was a disaster. Afterward, my emotions were badly askew as pain, anger, self-contempt, despair, and numbness vied for control of my heart. I went home a mess.

I talked with my wife about my feelings, and her caring calmed me enough to face them and listen. As I minded my emotions, I "heard" my pain telling me, "You confronted this woman because your goal was to help her align with truth. So far, so good. But you held back in your confronting, because your not-so-good goal was to keep from becoming too exposed, since her pain gave her the moral high ground. You didn't want to be wrong, because you believe that being wrong is *really* bad when it puts a strong woman in a position of judging you to be incompetent. Your fear of being exposed as incompetent keeps you from loving to the full. You still believe that risk-management behaviors can protect you more than God can. You believe that if you take risks, you'll be exposed as a nobody."

Listening to my emotions told me a lot — maybe more than I wanted! Yet I'm strangely comforted in seeing the darkness of some of my beliefs. That darkness makes me aware of the brightness of some of my other beliefs. For example, I believe that God is invading the world with a kingdom in which I am gifted and competent to serve him, to please him, to reveal his glory, to live in his light, to thrive in his love, to challenge the world around me, inviting others to know him and be known by him. As long as I desire God and listen to that desire, I'm going to be all right.

We are called on *by* God to bring everything within us *to* God, and this must include our emotions. Otherwise, we bring only a fragment of ourselves to the One who calls for all. Our emotions invite us to come under his Word with a stirred and open heart. Our emotions, again, are looking for words to say. The sooner we can find the words that properly express our emotions, the sooner we are ready to hear what God might say in response. The idea of finding words for our emotions gets to the heart of this book's title, *Minding Your Emotions*. Unless we can think toward the real message of our emotions (teaming up mind and feelings), large parts of our hearts will stay numb. These numb fragments remain unavailable to the healing, nourishing words of God that seek the whole of us in order to make us whole.

CHAPTER 7

Part One Summary

W e can't learn from denied emotions. So, obviously, living in a feeling-starved rationality won't do. That's when our boat has no sails. On the other hand, we can't learn from pure, ceaseless expression of our emotions, either. That's when our sailboat has no rudder and is driven before the wind. We've also seen that mere mood won't propel the boat any better than these other two options. Mood is like a dull, humid, listless breeze that makes sailing uncomfortable without appreciably moving the boat. We can't learn from mood, because it's too unfocused. Denied emotions, overexpressed emotions, mere mood — these cannot serve as the teachers God meant emotions to be.

God gives us the capacity to feel because feelings move us. God wants people who are on the move, not stuck, not dead, not passive. But he wants us to move *toward him*. This means that our emotions are not to move us to *direct* action but to learning that leads to *wise* action. When we pause to learn from our emotions, we find that there's a greater story than our own and that, through our emotions, it's beckoning to us.

Our emotions are meant to prevent our becoming stuck in the too limited story of our lives. The themes, dreams, and schemes of that story often plow a rut of sameness for us so that we're stuck for decades in the same old reactions to life. Our emotions, if we mind them, can pull us out of the rut. They tell us about significant changes in the relationship between our story and external circumstances. Our up emotions tell us that the world of circumstances is confirming our story. When this happens, we have a chance to learn how dependent we are on things going our way. Our down emotions tell us that the world of circumstances is contradicting our story. When this happens, we have a chance to learn anew that our hope is in God, not in circumstances. Either way, minding our emotions invites us to learn that God's greater story is inviting us to come within and dwell in a story that fills us with joy.

Learning from our emotions is intensified when our dreams and schemes are clobbered by the "givens" of life. The givens are things that just *are* (for example, a small engine repair will make you so crazy you won't know yourself). Givens can be amusing, but sometimes they're deadly serious. In chapter 3 I related them to Genesis 3. God brought curses into play as severe limiting factors meant to turn humankind away from self-sufficiency and back to him. Colliding with these limiting factors helps us listen to our hearts telling us how it feels to live in a fallen world.

The danger is that, instead of listening to our hearts, we'll lapse into a pervasive dulling of emotions that I've called *mood*. Mood isn't expressive and it tends to control others. It doesn't honor God, because its lack of focus ruins the potential for effective speech. It doesn't honor people, because it controls others. As such, then, mood is a violation of Christ's commands to "love the Lord your God with all your heart, and with all your soul, and with all your mind, and with all your strength" and to "love your neighbor as yourself" (Mark 12:30-31).

The way out of mood is not through expressing oneself but through using the *emotion cycle* (chapter 4). The cycle shouldn't be used mechanically, but rather should be seen as a start-anywhere-and-learn-from-there guide. The point of the guide is that our emotions exist within a context. Without understanding the context, it's hopeless to try to grasp the emotion itself.

Putting emotions in context also helps us deal wisely with our longings. The emotion cycle maps out, among other things, the intermittent conflict between stubborn truths and heart-desires. When emotions are intense, we're tempted to ditch the truth and satisfy our desires, consequences be hanged. This is disastrous, because desire, whether frustrated or fulfilled, is meant to lead us to God. Desire, rightly perceived, is the outstretched hand of God. On the other hand, squelched desires become perverted, shrunken wants that whiningly submit to the foul things the world offers as quick fixes.

Emotions, rightly minded, lead us toward God and away from those foul things. There are three basic ways of handling our emotions: stoic, ventilationist, and scriptural. In the stoic approach, the mind has overwhelmed our other God-given capacities (will, imagination, emotion). Ironically, the mind, while initially emphasized in this approach, ends up being weak. Apart from the passionate interaction among the other capacities, and between them and God, the mind becomes overwhelmed by the constant flux and threat of life. In the ventilationist approach, the emotions overwhelm all the other capacities. Competing passions result in chaos, covetousness, and murder (in many senses of that word).

Isaiah 55 outlines a scriptural approach built on the idea that the key to satisfied desire is listening to a Person. Listening to our emotions invites us to listen to God. Only he can address the messages of our emotions with kind, wise, and strong words that transform us from weary hearts into strong hearts. In our new strength we find deeper intimacy with God and new victories for him.

Now we turn to the emotions themselves. We'll look at five of the most dominant emotions of our culture: anger, grief, fear, shame, and joy. Each emotion should be minded in a slightly different way. I've concentrated more on the down emotions, because they more often carry us closer to despair, and our defenses against despair are often weak.

Part 2

Key Emotions and
How to Mind Them

CHAPTER 8

Anger — The Heart's Warrior

If handled properly, anger can be invaluable in opposing evil.

Today I expected a counselee to show up for a midafternoon appointment, two weeks after her previous appointment, just as usual. She didn't come. I sat alone in my office with the *tick, tick* of the clock. At fifteen minutes past her scheduled time, I called her to see where she was. "I've got you down for three o'clock today," I said.

I thought I'd hear an apologetic "I'll be right there." But instead she said, "No. Don't you remember? We said we'd meet a whole month from our last session. You even remarked that you thought I could handle a month between sessions."

It dawned on me that she was right. My mistake. Yet another mistake. Just a couple of days before, I had scheduled two people for the same appointment slot. Now I informed myself, *You're really cracking up!*

As I hung up the phone, I was angry. I still am. Let me analyze what, specifically, I'm angry about. Let's see:

▶ I'm angry at myself for making a mistake.
▶ I'm angry that others were unable to use the appointment time.

▶ I'm angry because my mistake deprived my family of income.

▶ I'm angry at myself for being angry.

What do these varieties of anger have in common? They all reflect unfulfilled longings. I long for a world where mistakes are no big deal. I long for a world that works better than this one. I long for a world where money no longer plays a vital role. I long for a world where I don't have to fear judgment — my own or others'.

What will prevent my being overwhelmed at the gap between the world in which I live and the world for which I yearn? Anger is the heart's warrior, springing to the forefront of the attack. Anger, properly used, protects my heart and others' hearts from being completely violated in a world where the wicked prosper.

Anger's Uses

My daughter comes home from school and announces that she missed making salutatorian for her graduating class by some tenths of a percent. Further, the guy who finished immediately ahead of her in the ranking is known by his fellow students as a chronic cheater. There's more: the cheater has been reported to various teachers on many occasions. Not only have these teachers done nothing effective in response, but the student has been rewarded for it in being honored as salutatorian.

My daughter is angry. Was it worth it for her not to cheat? Should she give in to temptation and hope to get rewarded as did her fellow student?

And I'm angry. Why should I raise my kids to do what's right when wrong wins out so easily? Why do I have to feel my child's suffering when it is so unnecessary?

As I sense my anger, I realize that I'm at a fork in the road. Down one path, I'm tempted to retreat into a pious shelter, that of "rising above" the anger with a philosophical response, something like "Someday this kid's conscience will awaken, and then he'll have to deal with a burdened heart." While this may be true, this response does nothing to show my daughter that someone is strong enough *now* to respond to injustice. Down the other path, I'm tempted to fly into a rage. I want to wipe the smug look off this young man's face as he strides forward to receive his award. Can this be a right spirit within me?

Surely there is a way between the alternatives of pious cowardice and rageful attack. How will I find this way? Already, my anger has accomplished something important by drawing this question out of me.

Anger makes me ask questions of my own heart. And as I ask these hard questions, I'm struck by my inadequacy in answering them. Ransacking my own intellect and experience, I sense that my resources are thin. I am reminded of Peter's words to Christ, "Lord, to whom would we go? You alone have the words that give eternal life" (John 6:68, NLT). I see where my anger-inspired questions are leading: to God.

Face to face with God (which is where I belong, anyway), I'm confronted with a heart whose inclinations are infinitely farther-ranging than my own. God's heart is inclined toward my daughter, but also toward the young man who cheated and toward the teachers who overlooked the cheating. God wants justice, but not naked justice. He wants justice compounded with mercy, as he says in Micah 6:8:

> He has told you, O man, what is good;
> And what does the LORD require of you
> But to do justice, to love kindness,
> And to walk humbly with your God?

Naked justice would reflect the same heartlessness as that of the character Javert in Victor Hugo's *Les Misérables*. Javert is the face of legalistic, merciless justice. At one point, though, Javert's life is spared by the man he has harassed and pursued for years, spared by a criminal whose heart has turned and become kind beyond measure. Javert has no capacity to understand that mercy could come to him from someone he himself has treated mercilessly. How could one who deserves no mercy be the source of lessons in mercy? Hugo describes Javert's struggle as "the throwing of a soul out of its path, the crushing of a probity irresistibly hurled in a straight line and breaking itself against God."[1] In his encounter with God, Javert is broken. In his brokenness, he has the chance to expand, to grow, to break out of the rigid confines of a calculating, law-ridden conscience.

In my own encounter with God, I, too, am broken. My anger has delivered hard questions into my heart. I have turned to God, not leaning on my own understanding, but seeking to trust in the Lord with all my heart (see Proverbs 3:5). I've had to face the flinty hatred within me that wants to turn "the wicked" into a category of nonhumans into which I can pour my rage. God has poured my hatred into the crucible of his love so that he can burn and purify my rage to see whether anything is left.

Is there anything left? Yes. I find that I'm still inclined to pursue justice, but this time, justice imbued with charity. I no longer want to grasp for an award for my daughter but rather to show her and all involved that there are bigger issues to face — the incursion of evil into the heart of a young man, the hope that he himself could find a better way, the hope that my daughter can learn to suffer well, the theme that God blesses those who follow him even when human institutions fail.

First, then, my anger has sent me to God. Now my anger, purified, leads me to think through how to interfere with evil, including the evil within myself. We've already seen how I could have used my anger to turn "the wicked" into a massive sponge for my hate. What I find evil within myself is my refusal to think of the cheater as the focus of God's love just as my daughter is the focus of mine. But God says, "Love your enemy," so whatever I do must be consistent with love.

Not only does anger move me to deal with evil in myself; it also moves me to hinder evil in others. When I explore God's anger at sin, I do not find the moody, flaring anger of a whim, but a righteous indignation burning against the sin that causes chaos. Once more, sin has released the virus of disorder into his beloved creation. God can't stand by and let this happen any more than an earthly father would allow a bully to assault his child. Anger is our protective response to the hearts of others, including the heart of the evildoer. Anger, when properly used, is the barricade between humanity and sin-driven chaos.

Can there be any question that this protective function of anger is vital? Is chaos not running wild in every corner of the world? Has chaos not invaded every relationship on the planet? Aren't chaotic relationships places of suffering? Isn't chaos the device of Satan, who turns everything upside-down, makes order impossible to attain, and pushes Christian spirituality into a private corner from which it cannot influence the public square? Once we answer these questions in the affirmative (as we should), we can see anger as a soldier in the war between God's kingdom and Satan's domain.

Anger thus pushes us to face the evil in fallen social structures, such as government, churches, commerce, the family, the military, and mass movements (like gay liberation, the Moral Majority, and so forth). Let's take the world of commerce, for example.

How much evil has been unleashed through the maxim that as each person pursues his or her self-interest, the good of all society is served? This is the central tenet of capitalism, and it went largely uncriticized by Western Christianity in the twentieth century. Sadly, in the words of theologian Lesslie Newbigin, the church has moved from the "assumption that economics is part of ethics and therefore depends upon theology, to the modern assumption that economics is an autonomous science with which theology has nothing to do."[2] The church, then, has failed to be prophetically critical of the surrounding culture. The church has failed to get properly angry at the incursion of sin into the realm of economics and commerce. The church has failed in its responsibility to declare the true basis for being human: "True freedom is not found by seeking to develop the powers of the self without limit, for the human person is not made for autonomy but for true relatedness in love and obedience; and this also entails the acceptance of limits as a necessary part of what it means to be human."[3]

A contrary example is that of William Wilberforce and the Clapham sect, a group of Christians who spearheaded the abolition of the slave trade in England early in the nineteenth century. Led by Wilberforce, the Claphamites were angered by sin's ugliness to the point that they persevered for decades until English slavery hit the barricade created by their anger and pain at the enslavement of fellow human beings.

As in this case, anger shakes us out of numbness and complacency. Left to ourselves, we're prone to drift into a comfort zone in which the only anger we feel occurs when someone disturbs our ease. But the Christian is not made for equilibrium. The Christian is to live under a call from God that sends him or her into arrhythmia. Honestly minding our emotions in a profound, untamed relationship with God — and doing this in the midst of a fallen world — is not an easy walk. Indeed, we should speak more of the "Christian lurch" than the "Christian walk." Skirting the edge of numbness one day, overcorrecting into despair the next, stumbling into rage the following day — all this makes for a careening journey of breathtaking highs and lows. Why are many Christians boring, "nice" people? Because they're living the Christian formula, not the Christian life. Life is dynamic, energetic, vigorous, vital. Jesus came that we might "have life, and have it to the full" (John 10:10, NIV).

Anger and Rage

Are you surprised that I've been describing anger in such positive terms? Isn't anger a bad thing? It can be, but its bad form is properly called rage. Rage is a debased type of anger that operates from wrong motives and produces ill effects. If you feel yourself tempted to cross the line from anger to rage, take a step back. "Be ye angry, and sin not" (Ephesians 4:26, KJV).

There's as much difference between anger and rage as between a dog's bark and its bite. Rage is not simply intensified anger.

Rather, anger and rage have entirely different objectives. Anger's goal is to protect from evil. Rage's goal is to avenge the fragile ego. Anger wants good as the final outcome. Rage wants to be rid of threat at all costs.

Let's differentiate between these two more fully.

Anger Is Based in Sadness; Rage Is Based in Anxiety

Anger gets jump-started when one realizes that sin is unchecked in some sphere of life. Because sin is often manifested through foolishness, we could say that anger grows in the soil of sadness at unchecked foolishness. Anger seeks to impose consequences on foolishness; otherwise, the fool will never experience enough pain to turn from foolish ways.

Rage, on the other hand, is not aimed at foolishness but at threats (real or imagined) to the insecure self. Rage is always evidence of anxiety. Rage erupts when one's frail sense of well-being is about to be overwhelmed by an outside agent. Rage is a defensive, last-ditch effort to restore that well-being.

Rage is illustrated in God's description of Edom in the book of Amos:

> He [Edom] pursued his brother with the sword,
> While he stifled his compassion;
> His anger also tore continually,
> And he maintained his fury forever. (1:11)

As we see plainly illustrated here, rage has an element of mercilessness.

Anger Is an Adult Emotion; Rage Is Infantile

When I'm angry at someone (as opposed to being enraged), I'm assuming that we're both adults and that we can reason through the issues that divide us. I never lose sight of the other or myself as a person. I don't turn the other into an object to be destroyed (as rage would), and I don't turn myself into an object of shame (that is, I "should" be ashamed for being angry).

Rage, however, is infantile in that it assumes that I'm small and insignificant and that no one must find out about my inadequacy. Rage is a blast of contemptuous force that intimidates the other so that he or she never comes close enough to see how small I am.

Anger Builds Up; Rage Tears Down

When anger has run its course, it wants both parties to be reconciled, to see both parties mature. Anger is an emotion based in hope. Anger wants to see things improve, to reach a higher plane, to reach for abundant life.

Rage isn't satisfied until the other has been reduced to powder. Rage is not about the removal of foolishness; rather, it is about the removal of the other who has become a threat. Rage ends in cutting off the other from all hope of relationship, the idea being that once you've hurt me, you can never again deserve admittance into my life.

Anger's Masks

Maybe you're not tempted by rage. You don't want to lash out and hurt just to make yourself feel better. But maybe you err in the other direction: you aren't willing to accept the burden of a proper anger. When a cause for anger arises, you put a mask on your emotion and try to make it appear as something else. You may not know you are doing this, or you may be aware of it and have what you think are excellent reasons for it. But if anger is the warrior among emotions, given to us by God to do battle with injustice, then putting a mask on it is nothing short of sinful.

Anger can be, and often is, masked by each of the following sins:

▶ *Niceness.* An example of this sin is the failure to confront someone who has hurt your child (assuming your child is too young to confront the other on his or her own). That may seem like a godly response (or actually, a nonresponse), but it is not. It may seem like the nice thing to do, but the Bible calls us to be kind, not nice. Niceness is a refusal to let someone inside our pleasing exterior. Niceness originates in shame ("No one must see what I'm like on the inside"). An honest expression of anger, not niceness, is called for in certain situations.

▶ *Emotional deadness.* An example is running away from feelings and calling it "stability." That's what happens when a woman ignores her husband's abuse of her, thinking she's doing what's for the best. But by squelching her feelings of hurt, she is actually making things worse for herself, diminishing herself. The phrase *unfeeling person* is an oxymoron since to not feel is to be less than a person. We need to allow ourselves to feel righteous anger.

▶ *Intellectual idolatry.* Here an example is assuming that a resourceful, well-informed mind is the only true key to Christian maturity. While a Christian mind, consistently thinking Christ's thoughts after him, is an indispensable asset, it cannot stand alone. It will inevitably be impoverished by its lack of interaction with the emotions. Having an isolated mind, untouched by passion, is a Greek — not biblical — idea.

▶ *Allowing oneself to become a dumping ground for others.* As an example of this, consider a husband who allows his wife to badger and belittle him constantly over their house (too small), their cars (too old), and their friends (too low-class). If he got a little angry at her unwifely behavior, maybe they could begin working toward a healthier relationship. He'd be doing his wife and himself a favor. Anger in this situation is entirely justified and likely beneficial.

▶ *Maintaining a chronic depressive mood.* For example, no one enjoys being around Uncle Ed because he's always sour and glowering. Nothing is any fun for him, and he rains on every parade he can find. If you ask him what's wrong, he'll say, "I'm just tired." In all likelihood, Uncle Ed is far more angry than he is tired. A suspended anger that stays inside, being fed through rehearsals of how unfair life is, will usually turn into rage.

Whenever we chronically avoid anger, we encourage evil. Evil recoils only when it runs into resistance. Anger is one form of resistance. (Of course, there are many other forms of resistance, such as extending surprising grace to one's enemies.) Withdrawing from anger leaves us and others unprotected. Anger insists that protection is vital and that loss of anger is a failure of one's duty to protect. But the safety that anger provides is not that sought by the fragile ego. Rather, the protection anger brings is grounded in concern for God's kingdom. Healthy, holy anger comes from seeing the world through God's eyes.

Anger and the Emotion Cycle

Tracing anger through the emotion cycle requires us to bring it out from behind its masks. Specifically, we should suspect chronic niceness, emotional deadness, overintellectualizing, and depressiveness of harboring anger. All four of these are efforts to bypass the heart, and this is one instance in which a heart bypass is clearly deadly. The problem with hiding anger behind these masks is that passive anger becomes fuel for self-pitying rehearsals about one's sorry lot.

Chronic niceness, for example, could lead to the following inner rehearsal: *I try and try to reach out to Mary, and she never reaches back. Maybe I'm missing the key somehow. Maybe I've offended her and I don't know it. The other day I was a bit down; maybe she took it for unfriendliness. I'll just work harder to win her over.* Meanwhile, Mary has no intention of being reached, so the cycle continues with mounting frustration and increasingly effortful niceness on the part of the pursuer.

Emotional deadness could bring on an inner rehearsal something like this: *Why don't I have more friends? We get to a certain point and they want to go deeper. Then I don't seem to have anything to give. They want to know where I am, what I feel. What's the big deal? Why can't friends just chitchat and let it be? But they want more, and I feel like a freak. Why can't I just be me?* This rehearsal hides an anger that intimacy requires more than giving your hands; you also have to give your heart. Maybe there's deep anger here, too, about a time when this person did offer her heart and had it smashed. Now she's furious that she may have to trust someone again if she's going to have real love in her life.

Overintellectualizing could bring on a rehearsal like this: *It's nice up here in my head. I get to analyze everything to pieces so that I'm ready for anything. Why should I come down from this tower? It's painful to be around people who think sloppily and wallow around in their emotionality. I reach in, not out. I sit in my observation post and see everything coming. I won't be surprised again.* Here is hidden anger at a world where surprises come readily.

Depressiveness contains rehearsals too: *I just can't seem to get interested in anything or anyone. I wish someone would notice. I wish my downcast face would serve as a signal that I need someone to rescue me. Then sometimes I wish everyone would go away. If people would just keep their distance, there would be no more losses.* Here is hidden anger at a world where losses come readily.

Distinguishing anger from its masks is similar to distinguishing focused emotion from mood. No one can benefit from using the emotion cycle until he or she admits emotions that are quite clear, if disturbing. Whether in the larger issue of separating focused emotion from vague mood, or the smaller but still crucial issue of separating anger from its masks, one must have the courage to face his heart. As David said to God after months of hidden guilt, "You desire truth in the innermost being" (Psalm 51:6).

CHAPTER 9

Fear — Warning of Danger

We become afraid when we doubt God's promises to take care of us.

"**D**addy!"

Daddy groans in his sleep but doesn't move.

"*Daddy!*"

Daddy cracks open an eye. *Where am I?* he wonders. He can't remember, although he feels he must have some obligation to the disturbance resounding in his head.

"*Da-a-addy!*"

"I'm coming," he mumbles, and pads toward what he hopes is the door. He begins to realize that the siren in his head is his four-year-old calling from her room. Loudly. He arrives at the siren's origin point. "What is it?"

The four-year-old is standing on her bed, backed into the corner. She points. "Something is in the closet, Daddy."

He turns on the closet light, finally awake, touched by her fear. He makes a big show of searching the closet. "There's nothing here, honey."

She shakes her head. "It might come back when you're gone."

He looks at her wide eyes and sees dread there. "Tell you what," he says: "I'll go get my pillow and some blankets, and I'll just curl up and sleep right in your closet. How's that?"

She brightens and relaxes. "Will you?"

"Yes."

"Oh, Daddy. That will be so safe for me."

"OK, honey. Safe you'll be."

Each of us is the little one standing on the bed, staring with dread into the closet. We have a deep, primitive fear that something out there is bigger, more terrible, and more predatory than we can begin to handle. Have you ever wondered why horror movies are so popular? It's because they speak to this archetypal fear that we are the hunted. In every horror movie the decent people become prey to something dreadful and aggressive. At the last minute some hero steps in to destroy the destroyer. We pay hundreds of millions of dollars each year to watch horror films because we need to see, over and over, that the predator is defeated.

The real predator suggested (unconsciously) in these movies is, of course, Satan. Even in secular America there's a dim awareness of threat beyond our control. This is the basis for all fear. Can you imagine the collective sigh of relief we'd all utter if God announced that he had decided to cast Satan (and with him, all harm) into the lake of fire ahead of schedule? As it is, Satan is still loose, and that is why we are all pressed into a corner, staring fearfully into the closet. When the dad offers to sleep in the closet, his daughter relaxes completely. The closet has been turned into a place of safety. *She* can't control whatever might be in the closet, but her strong daddy can. So she sleeps peacefully.

Another way to think about what's changed for the daughter is that her situation moved from an uncertain and scary outcome to one that was certain and safe. Her father's loving intervention transformed fear into peace. We're all desperately concerned for outcomes we envision as essential. We want our children to turn out well. We want the infertility to be cured. We want the cancer not to come back. We want the love we felt early in our marriage to return. We want a place to belong. We want to love and be loved.

Fear is an emotion we all know and all need to mind.

"You Don't Matter"

Fear has many faces, all of which seek a promise. Those faces include anxiety, worry, panic, self-consciousness, and phobias. Fear, in all its colors, can be thought of as posing a question: Is there a promise I can trust? If there is no answer to that question, or if the answer seems false, despair begins to burrow into the heart like a cankerworm. If there are no solid promises, how will I ever find safety? Promises are our great protection.

Despair says, "Your life is nothing, and every move you make to address the nothingness is also nothing." In other words, you can't get out of the corner where death reduces everything to a void. Despair says you don't matter in the least, nor do any of your efforts to matter really matter. If there are no promises that counteract the nothingness, then why stay alive? Why stay alive without any promises to stave off the despair that eats at our hearts?

Fear is the emotion we feel when despair's you-don't-matter message seems convincing. We desperately want to matter somehow. We want to do more than take up space; we want to connect with others, and we want to have an impact. So anything having to do with isolation (not connecting with others) or diminishment (having little or no impact) provokes fear. Death, since it brings both of these things (apart from faith in Christ), becomes an intense source of fear. Scripture reflects this when it says, "Therefore, since the children share in flesh and blood, He Himself [Jesus] likewise also partook of the same, that through death He might render powerless him who had the power of death, that is, the devil, and might free those who through fear of death were subject to slavery all their lives" (Hebrews 2:14-15).

Something in the human soul shrinks violently from death's power. Death is an allergen to the human heart, for death raises, as nothing else can, the question *Do I matter?* The fact that life is terminal collides with our need to extend, blossom, develop, grow. Death shouts, "You don't matter. You're a zero." We are in love with being and terrified of nonbeing. Why? Because as long as we continue to be, there is hope.

We hope that God will break forth from his unseen realm and collide with the present. We hope that the present is not just the latest deposit of the past but is (in theologian Jürgen Moltmann's words) "the front-line for the onset of the promised new life."[1] The word "promised" should jump out from this quote like lightning. This promise of new life reaches and touches the longing in our heart—the longing that includes wanting to keep on being but goes beyond that to a longing for safety.

We want something beyond mere existence. We want meaning; we want to be part of something worthwhile and fulfilling. No life can be satisfying as a mere function of length, even if it stretched into eternity. God's promises are the X-factor, the wild card that, once introduced, plasters this banner across all of life: "Behold, I make all things new." God's promises invite us beyond a lifeless life into vital, vigorous *living*. This vital living blossoms, pulses, extends, throws despair out of the heart. The promises of God give no place for "resignation, weariness, departure from the living hope. Despondence and despair are sin—indeed are the origin of all sins."[2]

Garden and Ghetto

What gives God's promises such power to touch us? Why do we need them so? The events of Genesis 3 suggest an answer. We might think of Adam and Eve's sin as exiling them from the garden into the ghetto. All of us are in the same dilemma as Adam and Eve: we're made for the garden, but we live in the ghetto. That is, we live in a fallen world that doesn't work very well, where relationships are too often places of suffering and where effort and results usually don't match up. There's a huge hollow in our lives that used to be filled with the joy of the garden.

Furthermore, the descent into the ghetto has darkened our minds, so we don't think clearly about how to respond to the garden-ghetto gap. Our fallen, foolish instinct is to close the gap between our longings and the tough world in which we live. We think we can erase the pain of being made for paradise and yet not living there.

We pursue two basic strategies to close the gap. First, we lower the garden, trying to make it more attainable by denying our deepest desires (that is, by shutting down our hearts, disowning the depth of what we really want). Second, we raise the ghetto by changing our world so that it *feels* more like the garden.

Lowering the Garden

This is the strategy of suffocating our longings. In effect, we're promising ourselves that if we don't expect much, we can bring about the fulfillment of our shrunken desires. We convince ourselves to live on crumbs.

Notice that the lower-the-garden strategy depends on three basic moves: First, I make a promise to myself (not consciously — I hold this move outside my awareness as I "suppress the truth in unrighteousness" [Romans 1:18]); second, I assess myself as having the resources to fulfill this promise; and third, I try not to dwell on the fact that what I'm promising myself will satisfy only as long as my heart is shut down.

How does a shut-down heart operate? By a sleight-of-hand, a ruse, a self-deception in which we exchange the truth of God for a lie and worship and serve the creature rather than the Creator (see Romans 1:25). In this exchange the created world is torn out of its proper place and elevated to do what only the Creator can do: bring life. As we load more and more of our demand for fulfillment on created things, including other people, they are drained more and more of irreplaceable resources. Since created things aren't designed to provide life and hope in themselves, the requirement that they do so exhausts them. We force legitimate but limited pleasures to disobey God by providing us with more than they are meant to give. The result: living becomes a wearying thing in a worn world. Everything smacks of fatigue as all creation cries out, "Depletion! Depletion! How long will you force us onward in the agony of attempting to fill your black hole of longing?" No wonder Paul writes that the creation is filled with "anxious longing" as it "groans and suffers" (Romans 8:19,22). A

111

shut-down heart leads to a depleted creation.

What greater indicator of this principle could there be than the environmental devastation that harries our planet? Environmental degeneration is a sign that creation has been called on to deliver gratifications that only the Creator can properly give.

Raising the Ghetto

The second strategy is to try to improve the ghetto so that it feels like home. Beneath this move is a legitimate understanding that we are made for a home. Homelessness is a form of diminishment we dread almost as much as death itself. We'll go to any length and take every possible measure to ensure an end to our homesickness. Whatever touches the ache for home becomes immune from critical examination. Once we feel a sense of "at-home-ness," we embrace with all our (shrunken) hearts whatever makes us feel that way. We become slaves to whatever lifts our mood. Unfortunately, those dependent on mood lifters seldom learn the art of adjusting their perspective. Instead of becoming big-picture thinkers and pray-ers, they end up enslaved to small, short-lived pleasures wrung out of an exhausted, weeping creation.

At this writing, I know of a seventeen-year-old who has abandoned his family to hang out with a group of troublemakers. Something about this group touches his aloneness, makes him feel embraced, and acts as an alternative to the love he wants. He's found his "home." He's made the ghetto feel a bit like the garden. No one will convince him otherwise. For now, he has conditioned his heart to want no more than the group provides. The pit feels like paradise, at least for now.

This young man has managed to shrink the space of pain — the gap between the garden and the ghetto — to a bearable size. The problem, though, is that his actions are accruing an emotional debt that must be paid in the future. Broken family relationships, self-hatred, eventual disappointment in his friends, an inflamed conscience, legal problems — the bill will certainly come due for all these things and more.

Earlier, I said we promise ourselves that shutting down our hearts will make life tolerable. Now, through the example of this adolescent, we can go on to see that we add another false promise: the created world has enough emotional resources to cure the homesickness in our hearts.

These are foolish, fruitless promises. The sooner we can face their sinfulness, the better for us. Otherwise, we'll continue to be tyrannized by an impossible task: mining this world for enough jewels to relieve the poverty inside us. More than that, we charge ourselves with the responsibility of making and keeping promises to ourselves—promises that load us and others with crushing burdens. The shut-down heart leads to a depleted world, as we've seen. Further, the depleted world raises the fear of exhausted resources, which drives us to greater efforts at self-sustenance and eventually self-exhaustion. In our anxiety and fatigue we must constantly monitor our hearts to see whether we've extracted enough from the world to fill the ache. We end up with what Martin Luther called "the heart curved inward upon itself."[3]

Promise Keeper

When our heart is curved inward upon itself because of the failure of the world to meet our ultimate needs, we are prone to fear. Remember, fear breaks into our hearts when despair says, "You don't matter."

The heart curved in on itself could be compared to a man pumping up a bicycle tire with a leak in it. A pressure gauge on the pump tells the man how he's doing. The deal is that if the gauge ever reaches zero, the man dies. He's tired, but he can't stop. To make matters worse, every so often a small bird with a sharp beak scurries to the tire and punches another hole in it. There are many of these birds, so the man must not only pump madly but also step on the birds whenever they come near. Meanwhile, he keeps a sharp eye on the pressure gauge.

This is a picture of the anxiety that saturates the human heart when we take responsibility for our own promise keeping.

Keeping our hearts reasonably filled with happiness is as hard as keeping the leaky, assaulted bicycle tire inflated. The hole in our hearts comes from the gap between the garden and the ghetto. The fact that this world is not our home punctures our hearts with a longing we try to fill from the very world that punctured us in the first place. A hopeless undertaking! What's more, the world is filled with aggressors who punch more holes in our hearts — holes like hopelessness, humiliation, disappointment, helplessness, broken dreams, betrayals, violated dignity, and failure.

Rather than face these realities, we glide past them in denial and continue to press frantically on the bicycle pump. Do we get tired? No problem. We recruit others to pump for us (never mind that they have their own hearts to fill). Or we trade off (I'll give you air if you give me air) and live off each other as parasites.

This parasitic living makes us still more prone to fear. For example, a married couple strikes a subtle bargain. The man wants to prove his worth through his work. He likes the idea of coming home to an orderly haven, but he's not particularly passionate about his wife. His wife wants the security of a good income, so she accepts this deal along with her part in it, which is to keep the home comfortably inviting and to raise the kids (in whom the man is mildly interested as long as their needs don't push him out of his comfort zone). No one says any of this out loud, but the bargain is struck nonetheless. This arrangement — and it is only an arrangement, not a relationship — works at first, but about ten years into it, the wife is getting tired. Her fatigue and anger don't get through to the husband, who just figures his wife is a witch. He's had his eye on an attractive younger woman at work anyway. In her, he finds a more efficient host to his parasitic needs and calls this discovery "love."

Imagine the fear within the wife's heart. As she descends into fatigue and frustration, and as her husband reveals his cluelessness and lack of interest in her pain, she realizes that she has nowhere to go. When she gets wind of his interest in a newer-model woman, she's paralyzed with anxiety. Her fear crescendos

114

when her husband's cell phone bill reveals many extended conversations with this woman, who looks more and more like a candidate for taking her once-comfortable life away from her.

The parasitic bargain this couple unconsciously arranged between themselves gave them no foundation for security. The promises they made before God at their wedding were emptied of meaning by an underlying arrangement that had more power and validity than any verbal commitment, no matter how laced with God-talk. The principle here is that unless we see and follow God as the faithful promise keeper, our selfish hearts will destroy each other in generating our own set of promises to ourselves. A corollary to this is that to the degree we generate our own promises and ignore God's, fear will dominate our lives.

To repeat: fear takes root when we buy into the you-don't-matter lie that Satan stabs into every heart. He tries to arrange life such that we feel a continual slide into insignificance. The smaller we feel, the more power he seems to have, until we're the four-year-old standing on the bed, staring and panicked. The intensity of this is too great, so we suppress it. But it leaks out in anxieties, panic attacks, phobias, and obsessive-compulsive disorders.

How do we respond to fear? By turning from our self-made promises and throwing ourselves wholeheartedly onto God's promises. We handle fear by going from self-made to God-made, from self-important to God-honoring, from self-satisfied to God-soaked, from self-preoccupied to God-dazzled. We must shift our primary attachment from ourselves to God, who says, "Abide in Me" (John 15:4).

The best way by far to see God as our protective daddy is to see Jesus up close. The Gospels paint a vivid, close-up portrait of Jesus. In those four biblical books God makes sure we are struck by the lightning of great stories and prostrated by the thunder of grand miracles. In that lightning and thunder dazzlement, we awake to Jesus etching true pictures of our Father on our hearts.

We can't drive out fear by pressing some "I will not be afraid" button inside ourselves. The only way to effectively drive out fear is to form a true picture of our Father. Given that Satan opposes our forming a right picture of God, we can assume that distortions exist in how we see our Father. For example, how did you respond to the opening story, especially when the father offered to sleep in the closet? Did you think that was too much? Impractical? Spoiling? Indulgent? Yet hasn't our heavenly Father gone much farther than sleeping in the closet? Hasn't he fought death, hell, sin, chaos, and Satan to a standstill so that all doors now open upon light, order, wholeness, glory, hope, and love? No matter how grim seems the maze we walk in this world, there is no path—for the believer in Christ—that leads to a fatal door. Unless our pictures of God direct us toward such safe thoughts, we must pray for discernment as to what our distorted image of God might be.[4]

CHAPTER 10

Shame — The Agony of Exposure

As people of faith, we need not wallow in shame over our failures.

William's torment is that he is alive. He had managed to keep this torment under wraps until one day when he finds himself alone and yet not alone. Flying at 20,000 feet in the cargo bay of a C-47, he's been surveying the contents of that bay for three hours. He isn't much interested in the obsolete jeep parts, the weapons up for refurbishing, or the crates of radio equipment. His eyes rest repeatedly on what gives him the most unrest: the six body bags. Six sets of human remains. He is flying back from Vietnam alive, and these men aren't.

He, too, had been fired on, but maybe he'd winced, turned, ducked. He imagines *them* moving face-first into harm. He'd taken cover. Prematurely? He can't tell. But them — obviously they had faced combat hell with courage. He sees them wrestling their way toward the enemy, fusing with the fusillade. Brave. They will never have to answer the accusation of cowardice that floods his mind with the noise of self-hatred.

One way to look at William's struggle is through the lens of shame. Why is William ashamed instead of elated to survive? To understand why shame is flaying his heart, we have to take a close look at what shame is.

Wreckage

In previous chapters we've seen that everyone, by virtue of being made in God's image, is endowed with two great longings: to contribute and to connect. We must return to these concepts in our attempt to understand shame. Both columns in the two following tables are important for understanding shame and the image-bearer, but we'll be focusing on the contribution column in each table.

Table 1: Fulfilled Longings

Contributing	Connecting
Feeling significant	Feeling secure
A sense of impact	A sense of intimacy
A sense of offering something valuable	A sense of giving and receiving hope
Passionate vision	Deep relationships
Making a difference	Delighting someone's heart
Dominion over the earth	"Naked and unashamed"
Gifted	Embraced
Honored	Safe in relationships

Table 2: Unfulfilled Longings

Cut off from contributing	Cut off from connecting
Feeling invisible	Feeling insecure in relationships
Feeling weightless	Feeling rejected and unwanted
A sense of having nothing to offer	Routine relationships
Making no difference	Unable to reach others' hearts
Feeling chronically overwhelmed	Feeling alone
Diminishment	Guardedness, defensiveness
Dishonored	Unsafe in relationships

The first table, "Fulfilled Longings," offers different facets through which to look at contributing and connecting. For example, you feel you're contributing when something you've said or done has a significant impact, really makes a difference. After all, we're all knights-errant at heart, longing to effect dazzling rescues, defeat fearsome dragons, turn the tide in favor of glorious causes. We want our names to be attached to something heroic. We want to give the counsel that saves the day, win the war for the cause about which we're passionate. And when the victory's won, we want to celebrate with others who fought the same good fight. We want to feast, sing, and dance. We want to enter the whimsical place of tale telling and experience the laughter that peals out the relief and pleasure of victory.

Recently, in a counseling session, an older gentleman — someone who could easily have excused himself as an old dog with no new tricks — turned passionately, decisively to his wife and made the heartfelt apology for which she'd yearned for over two years. Looking her dead in the eye, he brought their marriage back to life by offering soul-revealing sorrow. And she was thrilled. She accepted the apology as decisively as he gave it, and they held hands like teenagers for the rest of the session. At one point, the older man looked directly into my eyes and said, "Without your guidance, I'd never have been able to do this."

I flushed with pleasure. Why? Because he'd openly affirmed my significant contribution to their marital victory. I heard a message — partly from him and partly from God — saying, "You've made a real difference. You've contributed to a glad victory. Well done, my son." I felt honored, and my heart was lifted and blessed. But of course, the messages we receive are not always so affirming.

Let's go back to William in the C-47, sitting with his six mute accusers. Through them he hears, "William, you didn't contribute. You didn't pay the price. You flinched and looked after your own hide. We, the honored dead, are the judgment that you were willing to buy your safety through the sacrifices we made. You served no cause; you only served yourself. You are dishonored, and you can offer nothing to make up for your failure." William is breaking under the shame of these harsh, dark judgments, which are like millstones in his heart.

Now we can think of shame as the reaction we have when we hear (or think we hear) a message like this: "You are a failure and therefore lightweight, invisible, contemptible, negligible. You have nothing to offer — zero impact, zero contribution." Our shame is the wreckage of our longing for significance.

Writer John Eldredge tells the story of asking his son (aged six or so) what he wanted to do when he grew up. With shining eyes, the boy said, "Dad, when I grow up, I want to bring back the West."[1] In other words, he was saying that he had an adventurous spirit, and he wanted to use it up in service to a great cause. How will this boy avoid William's fate? How can he — or anyone — navigate toward the sea of honor and away from the shoals of shame?

Before we answer these questions, we must discern the difference between healthy shame and toxic shame.

Toxic Shame

Not all shame is bad. In fact, psychologist Lewis Smedes wrote, "Only a very noble being can feel shame. . . . If we feel like flawed persons it may be because we are in fact flawed. Our shame may be a painful signal that we are failing to be the persons we are meant to be and may therefore be the first hope of healing."[2] If I were to write bad checks as a way to rob others, I should feel ashamed. Shamelessness in the face of such moral failure would indicate a twisted heart. Shame becomes toxic only when it drives one to try to meet a standard that is not from God.

Recently, I collapsed in sadness, fatigue, and anger after weeks of nearly uninterrupted expenditure of energy. I was exhausted, then angry at myself for being exhausted. I was supposed to be — so I railed at myself — an iron man, able to push my way through anything that came at me. But then my wife pierced my angry darkness with these words: "You've been a warrior on many fronts. You've fought well. Now it's time to rest." Just like that, she exposed the toxicity of the shame that held me to a false standard. Her words were healing, honoring words, and they pulled my thorn of shame. They invited me to rest.

Now we can see that William, the Vietnam survivor, is struggling with toxic, not healthy, shame. Why is it so hard for him to rise above it? Why can't he open up to kind words from other places in his heart? Part of the answer must be that toxic shame finds ready-made handholds where prior shame has chiseled holes in the heart. Like a dormant virus, the early shame flares into fresh, searing life when new shame "wakes it up."

Early experiences of feeling flawed, helpless, or humiliated can quickly overload a child's heart. One man (we'll call him David) looks back in time and sees a young lad standing in a hallway and staring through the thin rectangle of a partly open door. David's drunken parents, as is their habit, have left the door ajar as they engage in sex. Only six years old, the boy is drawn to watch the shadowy figures and feels that he will never be strong enough or masculine enough to do whatever his father is doing to his mother.

Now, back in the present day, David would like to speak to himself as a boy and say, "Don't jump to conclusions about yourself. You don't have enough information to conclude that you're impotent and small. Just wait. Don't let this kind of scene tell you who you are." But no one is able to say these words to the boy, so he *does* jump to conclusions. He does feel small. He does feel he has nothing to offer. He is dwarfed by a standard that no boy is ready to meet — the standard of manhood — and he has no effective fathering to show him the way to manhood. So, being a man remains a mystery to him. He feels he doesn't have what it takes; he feels ashamed.

The shame in David's heart changes the meaning of many things. For example, he tries out for a baseball team when he's ten, but at the practices he sees a bunch of boys already doing manly things (batting, throwing, catching), and he figures he doesn't belong. There's nowhere for him to contribute on the baseball field (remember our longing to contribute?). In reality, he has just as much potential as the others, but this truth is hidden from him. The message of shame ("You don't have what it takes") is too strong. Shame loads normal challenges like this with more freight than is really there. Challenge, run through the machinery of shame, becomes the fear of diminishment. And diminishment becomes dishonor. One feels insignificant, and anxiety rushes in.

Years later, as a young man, David is in a corporate meeting where he's laboring to make a point in the presence of a sharp, critical older man. This situation is already a negative, shame-laced setting for the young man, who carries a long-entrenched struggle with dishonor ("You have nothing to offer"). He feels out on a limb. Still laboring, he makes a statement that the older man castigates. For a second, David can't see anyone from the neck up. He can't bear witnessing others witnessing his being dishonored.

The meaning of what the older man said has been changed in David's mind from "I question whether you've thought this through all the way" to "You have nothing to offer. You are as stupid as you feel." The power of shame lies in its ability to become a lens that tints and influences meanings, especially the meaning of events that remind us of earlier, toxic situations. Toxic shame changes meaning, discouraging and undermining all feelings of competence.

If someone feels mostly or totally incompetent, what's the cure? The cure is to realize that toxic shame is deceitful, that it hides the fact that one *can* make a valid offering in his or her world.

An Acceptable Offering

To understand this subject of making an acceptable offering, let's go back to a time shortly after Adam and Eve detonated the sin bomb that devastated all creation. The invasion of sin has separated Eve and Adam from God, from one another, and from their own selves. Nothing is whole anymore. The first pair have incurred God's curses and have been kicked out of their first home. They are now vagrant, homeless people.

But not all is wrecked, for Adam "had relations with his wife Eve, and she conceived and gave birth" (Genesis 4:1). In successive pregnancies, she bears Cain and then Abel. This is the third drama after the sin bomb explodes, and it is the first openly positive one. The first two dramas—confrontation with God (3:8-19) and banishment from the garden (3:21-24)—were unbearably sad, even though they contained seeds of hope.

New Life

This third drama starts out great: two births roundly declare that there's new life after the world's fall. And where there's new life, there's new hope. Eve realizes that new life is possible only with God's help and says, "I have gotten a manchild *with the help of the* LORD" (Genesis 4:1, emphasis added). After the terrible lapse recorded in Genesis 3, she finally acknowledges her dependence on God and testifies to the rest of us that we are needy and must, like her, turn to God for help and hope. This is her Magnificat.

As soon as new life enters the drama, a second scene is introduced. If the theme of scene one is "God is the author of new life in a sin-struck world," the theme of scene two is "New life is strengthened and preserved through offerings."

Lest we think this was an issue only for the ancients, let's remember our William, agonizing in the jump seat of an airplane's cargo bay because his offering could not match that of six men who gave their lives on the battlefield. The issue of offering is acutely modern. Every heart weighed down with shame has at its core the acidic despair of having nothing to offer. What else is inadequacy but the feeling that says, "What I have to offer is not enough"?

Cain and Abel—the representatives of new life—come to the crucial point of bringing their offerings to God. It's as if God is saying, "Now it's time to put new life to the test. The only way to

123

find out whether new life will endure is through its offerings." So Cain and Abel make their offerings.

Let's remember that these two aren't making their offerings in a vacuum. There's an important context in and around these acts of worship. First, human wickedness has destroyed the world. Second, God has made humans homeless. Third, new life is making the homelessness more bearable. Homelessness is beginning to yield to hope.

It's in the fragility of this setting that God comes near to respond to worship. Worship, then, is what will keep new life thriving. Worship will keep new life from straying back into the sin of self-sufficiency that so blinded Adam and Eve. Worship will continually win new life away from sin and chaos. Over and over, worship will bring hope to life.

But wait—worship must come from a right heart. Otherwise, it's just manipulation of God. Only a clean heart—one that has admitted sin and asked help for its wickedness—can become a source of God-pleasing worship, an acceptable offering. Jesus put it this way: "The true worshipers will worship the Father in spirit and truth; for such people the Father seeks to be His worshipers. God is spirit, and those who worship Him must worship in spirit and truth" (John 4:23-24).

God has been passionate about worship since the beginning. Worship is what Adam and Eve failed to do when God confronted them, and worship is what will divide Abel and Cain. True worship counteracts shame because it is the one offering that's always accepted. False worship deepens shame.

Lessons from Cain

The story of Cain and Abel provides a negative example that, when reversed, gives us a picture of a right heart. The darkness of Cain's heart points the way. From that dark heart we learn five essential things.

First, we learn how deeply we're designed for honor. Cain's enormous anger and discouragement arise out of his disappointment that "for Cain and for his offering [God] had no regard" (Genesis 4:5). Cain is shattered that God would not honor him. Do you sense within yourself how intensely you long for honor? This, too, is what Cain wants from God.

Second, God cannot honor worship when it's a screen for a selfish heart. Notice that 4:5 says that "for Cain and for his offering" God had no regard. It is *Cain himself* who receives no regard from God, and so naturally his offering meets the same fate.

Third, Cain's anger and "fallen countenance" reveal his smudge of a heart. The fallen countenance is a sign that Cain cannot meet God's eyes and is trying to hide his anger. Here, Cain lapses into the same sort of concealment as did Adam and Eve. Like them, he overestimates his cunning and underestimates God.

Fourth, a dark heart will become a questioned heart. Just as God asked Adam, "Where are you?" and asked Eve, "What is this you have done?" so he asks Cain, "Why are you angry? And why has your countenance fallen?" (3:9,13; 4:6). God exposes us with questions like searchlights into the dark sky of our fallen hearts. Do you sense him searching yours with his piercing questions? We live questioned lives, and the questions are salutary. They're meant to root out sin and shame and bring lightness and joy.

Fifth, God follows his questioning by offering Cain something to believe: "If you do well, surely you will be accepted. And if you do not do well, sin is crouching at the door; and its desire is for you, but you must master it" (4:7, NASB margin). What grace! Cain made a poor offering, yet God makes him a generous, good-faith offering in return. He returns good for evil. And how does Cain respond to God's gift? He kills Abel, his own brother. Essentially, he says, "I will *not* accept the humbling faith that would make me acceptable. I will not believe. I will concentrate on self-serving action. I will rise on my terms instead of bowing on God's." The violent, volatile vileness of such a heart was not created by God's refusal of the sacrifice but is revealed thereby and is the original basis for the refusal. While holding open the door of repentance,

God pushes Cain until the murderer in him comes out. It's as if God is saying, "Let me show you, Cain, why I didn't accept your offering."

An Offering of Faith

In Hebrews 11:4 we see the other side of this coin: "By faith Abel offered to God a better sacrifice than Cain." Because he had not walked in faith, Cain became a murderer. Because of such faith, Abel had developed a clean, worshipful heart, and his offering was accepted.

God isn't willing to distribute honor and regard indiscriminately. His regard goes to those who have faith in him (in New Testament terms, this would be called justification by faith). In God's pursuit of Cain he encouraged Cain not to waste time on anger and shame (fallen countenance) but to "do well" so that his shame could be taken away ("your countenance will be lifted up"). It's crucial to "do well" (get our hearts right, open and worshipful by faith), because the alternative is to continue with a hard heart ("if you do not do well"), in which case "sin is crouching at the door."

We learn from Genesis 4 that a human being is one who is called upon to contribute first to God. A human makes a valid offering, a true contribution in this world, when his or her heart has softened toward God in faith. No other offering can anchor the human heart in its longing to contribute. Similarly, Paul said, "If I give all my possessions to feed the poor, and if I surrender my body to be burned, but do not have love, it profits me nothing" (1 Corinthians 13:3). We could easily substitute "faith" for "love" in that verse since love is the relational form of faith. Apart from faith in God, all my contributions fall to the ground, for they are revealed to be coins spent to secure something for *me*. Apart from faith in God, then, all my efforts to cleanse myself from shame generate more shame because they harbor the prideful belief that I, an isolated self, can clean up my act through self-effort.

Now we can see that a vertical contribution (from us to God) of faith-generated worship leads to and hallows the horizontal contributions (from us to the world) that we make. When our mind is "set . . . on the things above" (see Colossians 3:2), we are blessed by God's reciprocal love and blessing, so that we find peace and wholeness. From this deep, secure place, our horizontal contributions lose their anxious, shame-bound agenda of filling our own emptiness. They become true, selfless offerings to others.

Resolution of Shame

William is only a fictional character I've created for illustrative purposes, but I feel sorry for him — I've left him suspended in midair, in midshame. I wonder what I would say to him if I could join him in the cargo bay of the C-47 for a talk. I think I might tell him a story that's found in the last chapter of John.

It was the time between Jesus' resurrection and his ascension to heaven. Jesus took this opportunity to tell the disciple Peter what kind of death Peter could expect. It would be a difficult martyrdom (John 21:18).

Then Peter did a surprising thing. He turned anxiously and asked, "Lord, and what about this man?" (verse 21), referring to his fellow disciple, John. In other words, he was saying, "You aren't going to make me go through a hard time and let John off easy, are you?" The implication is this: "I can stand my pain only if I'm not alone in it."

Jesus said to him, "If I want him to remain until I come, what is that to you? You follow Me!" (verse 22). In effect, Jesus was saying, "As long as I keep my promises to you, Peter, my plans for John shouldn't concern you. Accept your end. Relinquish control. I'll take care of you, and I'll take care of John on his different path."

I think William might be astonished at this story. He would understand very well that some people follow a life trajectory that takes them to an early death, while other people have a trajectory that continues on for longer. The shame could now slide off him. He could trust that he had permission to go on to whatever end his life would have, confident that he would find honor in whatever ending Jesus might accompany him to. The six body bags were not his judges but rather were like Peter, in whose death Jesus was somehow attendant. Jesus' relationship with all death and with all life could free William to follow, like John, a different path toward honor.

CHAPTER 11

Sadness — A Feeling
for What's Missing

> We react with sorrow to the losses that happen
> in a world accursed.

L oss and gain are big deals to us. Take unemployment, for example. Right now, all over the world, many are dealing with the recent loss of their jobs. And they're dealing with it in any number of ways. Some of them are sitting by themselves, feeling stunned; some of them are getting drunk; some are on their knees; some are talking it over with a friend; some are pounding the table in rage; some are stuffing every feeling. But very few can shrug it off.

Loss is big. Gain is big. Why? I think it's because they are a lot like blessings and curses.

Blessings and curses are diametrical opposites. Blessing is like coming home; cursing is like being evicted. Blessing is about being soaked in God's generosity, so that happiness and prosperity come. As Jürgen Moltmann says, blessing means "there is enough to go around."[1] Cursing is about being lost amid depletion, desolation, and poverty. There is not enough to go around; there is not even enough for oneself. Loss says, "You see? Life is a dreary descent into distress, with increasingly less and increasingly colder comfort along the way."

Loss makes us antsy because it reminds us of the power of the curses in Genesis 3. Whether the subtraction has to do with friends, relatives, years, accomplishments, looks, money, or fame, the effect is the same — we're being stripped of protection (or at least the illusion of it) against the curse (which is ultimate loss).

Blessing embraces everything that is meant by the Hebrew word *shalom* (peace, wholeness, well-being). Blessing brings life to its full, brimming vitality. Blessing comes from God through obedience: "Choose life in order that you may live, you and your descendants, by loving the LORD your God, by obeying His voice, and by holding fast to Him" (Deuteronomy 30:19-20). Thus, obedience, blessing, and life are all interconnected.

In contrast, cursing expresses all we associate with God's wrath: sickness, failure, ruin, abandonment, death. Is it any wonder that our emotions register our losses in a powerful way? Sadness is the heart crying out that loss is unendurable and that, unless help should come, the loss will break it.

Sarah's Story

An old woman living out her last months in decrepitude and dependence, Sarah has arrived at the sort of condition of life that makes most of us fear aging. When dentureless, her mouth makes a sunken wedge between promontories of nose and chin. She's marooned on a two-and-a-half-by-six-foot rectangle, her bed. Her glottal control is poor, so there can be no thought of a sip of water — every liquid has to be custard-thick before she can have it. Unthickened water would go directly to her lungs, drastically increasing her risk of pneumonia. So a drink of water becomes a spoonful of cloudy pudding fed to her by someone else (her coordination is too bad for her to feed herself). Meanwhile, she speaks labored words through uncooperative lips. Just as labored is her breathing as she fights to open her lungs, which are like a rusty bellows.

Some comfort there would be in all this if the setting was her home with family doing the caring. But she lies in a nursing home that smells of urine. She herself wears a diaper. For her, family contact is sparse. She has two children who live nearby, but somehow she's become invisible to them. She has seen her son once in six months; her daughter comes maybe once a month.

She is not well and she is not loved as she'd like to be, yet she is content. Her gains are few, yet they outweigh her staggering losses. She can barely speak, yet it's the fact that she's spoken to that revives her heart. She loves the biblical promise that says,

> He will feed His flock like a shepherd;
> He will gather the lambs with His arm,
> And carry them in His bosom,
> And gently lead those who are with young.
> (Isaiah 40:11, NKJV)

These words contain a gain for her that she'll stack up against any number of losses.

Yet look at the losses — loss of mobility, loss of coordination, loss of dignity through being radically dependent, loss of freedom, loss of family, loss of comforting surroundings, loss of teeth, loss of bladder control, loss of self-care abilities, loss of ability to express her wit, loss of freedom to attend her much-loved church. How can contentment thrive among all these weeds? It seems impossible, but it's enough for her that the Life-giver has promised to carry her in his arms. Jesus' love and his promises to her are bedrock.

In the spiritual classic *Pilgrim's Progress,* cast in the form of a dream, John Bunyan captured the steadying effects of Christ's promises. At a certain point in his "progress," Christian, along with his companion Hopeful, is crossing a river and feels himself in danger of drowning.

> Then I saw in my dream that Christian was as in a muse awhile, to whom also Hopeful added this word, "Be of good cheer, Jesus Christ maketh thee whole"; and with that Christian [broke] out with a loud voice, "O, I see

Him again! and He tells me, 'When thou passest through the waters, I will be with thee; and through the rivers, they shall not overflow thee'" (Isa. 43:2). Then they took both courage, and the enemy was after that as still as a stone, until they were gone over. Christian therefore presently found ground to stand upon; and so it followed that the rest of the river was but shallow.[2]

Lying on your back in a nursing home, virtually abandoned by your family, you either succumb to your catastrophic losses or you find "ground to stand upon" and fasten your heart to the promises of the One who has defeated the greatest loss of all: death. If the worst loss has suffered loss, can gain be far off? If death has died, if defeat is defeated, can Christ not mean to bless us and bring us to the other side?

Reasons for Sadness

Though Christ has lifted us on high through his promises, as Sarah has discovered, there are legitimate reasons for Christians to be sad. I can think of at least four.

Christians May Be Sad That We're Not Yet Home

This is the sadness of delay. Christians are constantly called upon to wait. We anticipate a breathtaking gain, but while we live in the light of it, we don't live in it.

Christians are like someone who waits outside a popular restaurant for an hour just to get a menu. We're still outside, but unlike many, we have a menu. And what a menu! Perusing it, we see why the wait for a table will be a long while yet. The food is delectably presented, both pictorially and descriptively. We can taste it, almost, with our eyes. We're enraptured! But then, after a while, all the joy winds down like someone turned off an old stereo with the needle still on the record. Devolving from antici-patory ecstasy, those of us outside the restaurant say, "We'd rather have the food than a million menus!"

Of course, this parable isn't perfect. Christians *do* have bits of the food of heaven: the indwelling Holy Spirit, degrees of freedom from the power of sin, opportunities to do God's will, a new identity in Christ, spiritual gifts, fellowship with other believers, to name a few. Yes, Christians have more than the menu.

Yet the chasm between earth and heaven is wide. Paul said, for example, that the "weight of glory" promised us in heaven is far beyond our imagination (2 Corinthians 4:17). He also said that to meet Christ after death is "very much better" than remaining on earth (Philippians 1:23). Similarly, John described a new creation where the curse will no longer be operative, where "there will no longer be any death; there will no longer be any mourning, or crying, or pain" (Revelation 21:4).

When we reach heaven, we'll be struck by how small were the supply drops of blessing on which we survived during our earthly journey. The contrast will be a shock, not because the supply drops from God's helicopter were skimpy, but because the generosity of heaven will be ultra-hyper-superabundant. It's this overflowing that we long for. Our hearts yearn for plenty and wrestle with the question "Is it wrong to want more?"

God's response is "No, it's not wrong. You're designed for more, but it's not yet time to receive the 'more.' In your present frame, the 'more' I have for you would overcome you. You must wait." It's this call to wait that makes our hearts sad.

Blessing is real in this life, but it is not complete. If God were to give us all he has right now, it would be like drinking out of a fire hydrant — overwhelming and even damaging. For now, we're called to live in the gap between what we're made for and what we can handle. It could also be thought of as the gap between our longings and our limits.

In his book *Theology of Hope*, Jürgen Moltmann says, "God is not first known at the end of history, but in the midst of history while it is in the making, remains open and depends on the play of [his] promises."[3] The phrase "the play of his promises" attracts my heart. It tells me of an interplay and dynamism among God's promises. A network of promise surrounds my life, and while God's promises are not yet fully fulfilled, there is enough completion of them in this life to give me a fabric of hope to wrap myself in. This fabric of hope becomes a shield against despair, even as sadness touches my heart.

Earlier, I called this the sadness of delay and the sadness of waiting. Waiting for what? Waiting to arrive home. There are days when I'm just ready to be home — no more of this sorrowful journey. Other days, the hope of heaven pulses brighter, transforming the sadness of delay until it becomes a sorrow that sparkles. Since my sadness is homesickness, my heart has space to heal.

Christians May Be Sad When Recognizing Difficult Truths
This is sadness at distortion and self-deceit.

Jesus' own sadness turns in this direction at times. In Matthew 23:37 we read how his heart reached a high tide of grief when he said, "Jerusalem, Jerusalem, who kills the prophets and stones those who are sent to her! How often I wanted to gather your children together, the way a hen gathers her chicks under her wings, and you were unwilling." His anguish bellowed against and battered the blindness of his people. His sadness was a passionate blow at a nation that had chosen darkness and had become comfortable with it.

Recently, a woman I know was reflecting on an evil in her family that had been hidden since she was a child: her mother's sexual abuse of her. While she had never denied the factuality of those events, she *had* denied their horror. For years. She had been holding down, with all her strength, an unbearable sadness. But she'd also known Christ for two decades, and she knew his work in her heart had been gradually increasing. When Christ came to knock on the door of her deep sadness, she sensed his saying, "It's time to face it." So she relaxed her stranglehold on her sadness and let it roam free.

She had thought that if her heart were free, if the sadness escaped her death grip, it would destroy her. Instead, she was shocked to discover that the sadness had a message for her. It was something like this: "I am the apostle of your broken heart. I am sent to tell you that it's time to heal the break between the competent, efficient adult you and the part of you that you left behind in order to survive the abuse."

The woman realized, over time, that she had turned away from herself as a child-who-suffered to build an adult-who-had-it-together. She blamed her suffering self for being weak, pursued toughness as a shield, and became a brittle, distant, unfeminine woman. Heeding the call of her sadness, she now turned toward the child-who-suffered and saw not weakness but horror. The denial was broken: she saw the self-blame, the self-hatred, and the misery in her soul. Now she was in a position to deal with what was real (the horror) rather than unreal (the illusion of self-sufficiency through toughness).

For this woman, listening to her sadness broke decades of denial. Many of us, likewise, are engaging in denial that we could put away if we would only listen to our sadness.

Christians May Be Sad with a Godly Sorrow

This is the sadness of contrition. Godly sorrow is a sadness over sin that leads, not to the place I'll call the whipping post, but to the cross. The whipping post is where we go to punish ourselves for our sins.

Let's say I fail one of my friends by demanding my own way in a trivial matter. When I realize my failure (or my friend points it out), I go to the whipping post by hurling abuse at myself, tying myself to the bad outcome so that I am the outcome — if it's bad, I'm bad.[4] When I see myself as irredeemably bad, my only recourse is to punish myself. If I can enter a relationship with myself where there is no mercy, perhaps justice can eventually be satisfied. The problem is, as long as I isolate myself at the whipping post, there's no standard by which that satisfaction can be measured. So I just keep flogging myself. This lifestyle can become so deeply ingrained that I stop grasping how abnormal it is to live with constant self-criticism. By then, the whipping post feels so familiar that I mistake it for "home" and "normal."

The cross is the center of a completely different atmosphere. We can imagine its horizontal beam as arms thrown wide to receive sinners, to free us from the penalty of our sins and bring us into the place of no condemnation. When we sin against and hurt our fellows, we're at a fork in the road: either we head to the whipping post with our grim determination to act as the law against ourselves, or we run to the cross, where heavy-heartedness encounters lightheartedness. The advent of God's lighthearted-ness at the cross does not minimize sin. It does, however, put the sinner on speaking terms with hope. And this "hope does not disappoint" (Romans 5:5).

At the cross all disappointment (including disappointment with ourselves) is made the prisoner of hope. Hope binds and limits the power of disappointment and turns it toward God's service. Disappointment becomes a journey toward the cross, a journey toward spiritual safety and sanity, a journey of regrets turned into reminders of God's grace and love. And God's love is greater than our fathom rope can plumb. The novelist Iris Murdoch says, "The point is, one will never get to the end of [God's love], never get to the bottom of it, never, never, never. And never, never, never, is what you must take for your shield and your most glorious promise."[5] Again, the outcome is a sorrow that sparkles.

Christians May Be Sad at the Rupture of Relationships

This is the sadness of separation. The core truth undergirding this principle is that God exists as a Trinity. Trinitarian theology misses the point if it tries to explain the Trinity and stops there instead of going on to apply the Trinity. The fact that God is three persons in a single, undivided essence calls us toward unguarded relation-ships. We are meant to connect so deeply that we are in danger of fusing with the other person. Yet our always referring back to com-munion with God pulls us away from fusion with others, while pre-serving a barely balanced intimacy between us. We hover between fusion and distance at the vulnerable place of agape love.

Trinitarian theology means that Christian disciples can never be indifferent to failed relationships. The one relational rupture approved by the Father was that between himself and his Son at the cross. Since in this rupture the Father made sin his problem and resolved it through the sacrifice of his Son, no other relationship need be broken. The one relationship that should never have been broken was broken voluntarily so that all relationships have the freedom to heal. Father and Son entered a relational cataclysm as a free, gracious offering of love that has the power to draw the poison out of every relationship, whether between individuals, ethnic groups, races, the sexes, or nations.

That relationships are entered into casually and discarded callously should provoke sadness in the believer. Our heads should be bent in sorrow at the relational carnage in our lives. Western culture has wrongly, horribly separated love and suffering, which are meant to exist together. One cannot love without suffering, because the main concern of love is the well-being (peace, wholeness, and aliveness) of the other. To the extent that the other walks in anxiety, fragmentation, and deadness, we suffer. This is not to exalt suffering as a thing in itself but to commend the suffering that comes when love meets resistance or disappointment and yet does not withdraw.

The condition of human relationships should always draw our concern and sorrow. Author Frank Laubach said, "Lord, forgive us for looking at the world with dry eyes."[6] If we Christians aren't saddened by the pandemic of exploitative, manipulative, power-obsessed relationships, our hearts are dead. Can we really be Christians and not weep over the suffering in relationships? Pray for sadness. Look at your own relationships. Pray for sadness again. Pray for a heart like God's as he labors over his benighted world.

Sadness's Uses

Earlier, we saw that gain and loss are significant because they are related to blessing and curse. Sadness reminds us of the power of

God's curse on the world and our helplessness in the face of that curse. Sadness takes us into helplessness and stills us as we grieve over our own foolish attempts to remake the world according to our own specifications. Sadness conducts us on a tour of our arrogant efforts at being the creator of our own "new" world rather than being merely a creature. Jesus, the "man of sorrows" (Isaiah 53:3), was the One who was "humble, and mounted on a donkey" (Zechariah 9:9). Sadness reminds us that humility is our proper station. What "donkeys" have I refused in my arrogance?

I need more of this constructive sadness in my self-deceived heart. Sadness is like a centrifuge that spins my heart around until it extrudes honesty. In that honesty I see both my own darkness and God's bright grace. That grace overwhelms me and arouses me to joy.

CHAPTER 12

Joy—The Dawn of Glory

In joy we experience an intense sampling of what God has in store for us.

Imagine that you're in heaven, walking between long tables at a feast. The sumptuousness, festivity, and rejoicing are beyond those of any party you ever enjoyed on earth. A vast company has gathered, the tables extending beyond the limits of sight in all directions. Your eyes flicker from one person to another—all are reveling, merry, relieved, surprised, restful, delighted, at peace. Some get up to dance. Some embrace. Some excitedly tell stories, while others respectfully and eagerly listen. Worship pervades all and interlaces one heart with another, and all hearts to the One.

Now your eyes are returning to one woman whom you'd barely noticed as you scanned the guests. What is it about her? At first, you think she's strikingly beautiful in the conventional way of earth—a magazine-cover face. Then you realize your eyes aren't engrossed in facial surfaces but in something deeper. This isn't a face invaded and held in place from outside by devouring glances. No, this face is transformed by an internal vigor, an energy forming it as if rising up from creative depths—caverns below caverns—that open out onto the heart of God. You realize you're looking on a beauty, not of surfaces, but of depths. You understand that you're looking on a beauty that you can't possess but that possesses something you long to possess.

Then you find yourself saying, "I know her!" Yes, you know her from the sidewalk the "shopping cart ladies" of your city would shamble down. Or from the mission where you would ladle out soup for the homeless. Or from the nursing home for the indigent where you would volunteer your time. It was in that place — wherever it was on earth where she spent her hard, later years — that she began to lay the foundation for this radiant beauty. Through the grace of suffering, she began to build, as it were, the muscles with which to lift this weight of beauty, lift it and carry it as she carries it now to you. As she blesses you with it, you see that every shimmer of her glory has, at its center and as its anchor, a scar. Not one scar, not one sorrow has escaped beauty's capture. Every loss has been subdued and turned, as a tamed creature, to the service of this beauty. Every ugliness in her life takes its place humbly and gladly, coming to rest as the servant of beauty.

The joy she'd known even amid the hardships of her life on earth had been a foretaste and a foretelling of the glory she now radiates like a sun.

Sown Hope, Harvested Joy

An enormous chasm lies between promise and possession. I've written about the heavenly banquet as if we already possess it, but the whole problem with our life on earth is that we live in the gap between desperately wanting our home and actually having it. Our hearts strain to lay hold of heaven. But the passion of our hearts, no matter how strong, has no power to bring heaven to us now. So, what do we do? Discard our yearning? Live with a death inside? No! Lacking possession as we do now, our hearts must focus their passionate desire, not on possession yet, but on promise.

If God is a promising God, we can afford to live passionately. If God promises nothing, or if he breaks his promises, then by all means, let's kill all passion in ourselves. Let's murder our hearts! Let's grab cheap substitutes for passion, lifeless things that we fantasize are charged with life. Let's ignore Ecclesiastes and rummage all through the earth for the illusion of life.

But if God is faithful to his promises, then we can say with Paul, "I do not regard myself as having laid hold of it yet [I don't have possession]; but one thing I do: forgetting what lies behind and reaching forward to what lies ahead, I press on toward the goal [I have passion] for the prize of the upward call of God in Christ Jesus [the promises are in a Person]" (Philippians 3:13-14). Paul, in love with a faithful Person who had made promises, was a passionate man. Earlier, he said, "I press on so that I may lay hold of that for which also I was laid hold of by Christ Jesus" (verse 12).

What a magnificent heart pulses in these verses: "one thing I do," "I press on," "reaching forward." Here is a man straining every cell to stay on track and reach the finish line. Is this the philosophy of a self-made man? Is this look-what-I-did masking itself with piety? No. Paul's passion was rooted, not in self-will, but in the prior, pursuing will of a loving, faithful Person: "I was laid hold of by Christ Jesus." Paul did not possess heaven yet, but he had been possessed by God. Paul was impassioned because the One who had him *would* give him all he had. The One who held him would not withhold from him.

A Person making promises is the bridge between now (no possession) and not-yet (full possession). Listening to this Person's good news and believing it — this brings hope. Hope is a promise made *and believed.* Hope comes when the circuit between heaven and earth is completed. When heaven's offer (promise) is truly received (faith), then hope is born. When hope is fully grown, it generates its own offspring: joy.

When I was a kid, my Great-Uncle Marvin, every Christmas Eve, would pull my brother and me aside and say, "Did you boys hear the news?" We'd stare at him; we didn't yet know what the word "news" meant. "Well," he'd continue, "the radio reports that Santa Claus's sleigh was in a wreck. Santa went into a ditch and broke his leg and can't climb down any chimneys. Looks like there won't be any Christmas this year." We knew what *that* meant, and the first year or two he said it, our hopes were dashed and our joy faded. In later years we bore with him knowingly and lost no joy. Why? Because our hope was strong that Christmas would come, for it always did, Marvin's gloomy rumors notwithstanding. Our hope had become full grown, and our joy could not be contested.

Story and Joy

Marvin accosted us every Christmas with a story. At first, we did not have a counterstory strong enough to recharge our hopes when his story dashed them. We had no story strong enough to support joy. But as time went on, we had greater evidence that Christmas was more secure than Santa's driving skills. This evidence led us to tell a counterstory, one we believed, based on that evidence. Confident expectation of Christmas was warranted, and so we had joy each year before Christmas ever came.

Human beings are creatures of the story of a relationship, which is to say, a story about love. Without love, there can be no happy ending and thus no worthwhile story. On the other hand, without story, there can be no love, for love is dynamic, not static. There has to be a plot or else love can't breathe and grow. If there is no story, we are unloved; if there is no love, the story dies.

Joy, too, breathes and grows in story. Joy requires the telling of a story, at the heart of which is a Person who, because he loves us, makes and keeps promises. Joy is about breaking faith with an old story and trusting a new one, the one God is telling. His story is about Immanuel, the nearness of God, given to draw us to God's full, glorious presence.

But there are competing stories that draw us away from God, from hope, from joy. These competitors are strong. How do we hold on to, and indeed strengthen our grip on, God's story — and therefore on joy?

We Live in the Story of Joy with the Help of the Holy Spirit

Between the time of promise and full possession, the story includes a present Helper, One who journeys with us in the gap. This is the

Holy Spirit, who keeps reinforcing God's story in spite of all competitors. Of him, Jesus said, "The Helper, the Holy Spirit, whom the Father will send in My name, He will teach you all things, and bring to your remembrance all that I said to you" (John 14:26). Jesus was speaking to the disciples about how they would remember, years later, what to record about him. But the theme of the verse applies to every Christian. The Holy Spirit will teach you and help you remember what is vital—this is the heart of what Jesus was saying.

Just as vital is the Spirit's assisting us to tell our stories to God (prayer) and to others (fellowship). If we don't relate our stories to others, our hearts die. Storyteller Richard Stone said, "Representing our world to others through story is innately human, as crucial to our soul's survival as breathing is to the survival of our body. Short-circuit this natural process and you will witness all forms of disease."[1] Relating our stories to God is part of what prayer is all about. What was Jesus doing in Gethsemane but telling his Father the story of his struggle to take the final steps to the cross? After he poured out his heart, he was able to say, "Nevertheless not my will, but thine, be done" (Luke 22:42, KJV). Later, we learn that it was "for the joy that was set before him" that Christ endured the shame of the cross (Hebrews 12:2, KJV). Could it be that his Father emphatically put that joy before him as he cried out in Gethsemane?

Unless we pour out our stories—good, bad, and indifferent—to our Father, it will be tough for us to see how relevant his story is. Many Christians have little real joy because they've never related God's story to their own. They've heard elements of God's story a thousand times ("Moses in the bulrushes—isn't that sweet"). But without imagination, the stories tend to become dead information to be stored in one's mental hard drive. Do we really think God takes the trouble to share his stories with us just so we can win at Bible trivia? No. He shares his stories to prove to us that his is the love we've searched for all our lives.

God aims his stories straight at our struggling hearts like sunlight aims at a budding flower. Problem: if we've never explored our stories, our hearts stay shut like a flower kept in darkness. It takes a lot of energy to conceal our stories from ourselves.

Recently, a troubled man spoke with me about his sexual addiction: he would repeatedly resort to homosexual pornography and imaginings. This man is a Christian, yet the living out of his faith was constantly defeated by his forays into sexual sin. And so we began to piece together his story. A major theme in this man's story, based largely in his relationships with his parents, was his fear of being absorbed by a powerful woman and abandoned by a weak man. His own masculinity seemed like a small stick as compared with the consuming fire of femininity. His dream, then, centered on a world where he'd be safe from feminine absorption. His schemes involved fantasizing about sex with men (because men don't absorb men, he thought) or about taking the feminine role in sex (because men don't absorb women).

Only when his story was out in the open could we begin to relate it to God's story in a way that awakened his heart. Specific elements of God's story that captured and revived his heart included these:

▶ That he had nothing to fear from true femininity
▶ That the women in his life had hurt him, not because they were female, but because they had failed to live out their femininity
▶ That God gave man and woman to each other as gifts
▶ That masculinity can be enjoyed and fully developed only in the presence of femininity

Embracing these truths opened his heart to God's story. Before, God's story could not reach his own, because he'd concluded that nothing in Scripture touched his deep fear that women were toxic and devouring. Until he consciously put together his story, he didn't even *know* he was afraid of women. How could God get through to him with the message "You need not fear women" when this poor fellow didn't even know he needed to hear it?

Story opens us up to hear from God. Moreover, God is telling stories in Scripture as connecting points with our own stories. The story of Noah's ark, for example, is for times in our lives when we feel rudderless (the ark had no rudder). Joseph's story is for times we've been falsely accused or when we've been betrayed or when we are in a hopeless pit. Of course, these stories and others in the Bible are historically, factually true, and that's important too. Myths are simply wishful thinking and are not powerful enough to sustain life. We need *true* stories, events that happened in space and time, and God has given them to us in his Word. But they're not meant to stay merely factual; they're meant to open our imagination.

We Live in the Story of Joy with the Help of the Church

God's community—the church—reveals Christ to the world by living out unconditional love in uncommon relationships. Just as Christ is the loving neighbor embodied in the Good Samaritan, so his church is to be this kind of neighbor within its own fellowship and to the observing world. The true neighbor is one who crosses fearful boundaries, gets outside his comfort zone, sacrifices his own time and goods, reaches out to the poor and downcast, brings healing, and makes a long-term commitment to the needy one.

The church, then, is meant to be a connected community instead of a collection of unrelated smiley faces. What is wrong with the phony, smiley-face church? People aren't telling their real stories, and no one is listening to anyone else. A thick smoke (caused by the friction of nonneighbors rubbing up against each other in aggression) hides the hearts of many. Or a syrupy sweetness (generated by a desperate pressure to fit in and belong) sticks everyone together. When most are either attacking (the smoldering friction) or withdrawing (into the syrupy sweetness), no real stories can emerge. The false stories of "I'm the angry victim" or "I'm always fine" conceal our real stories and shut down our hearts.

The church is meant to be a community where our stories come out and encounter God's story. Joy grows as we grasp that nothing in our story can escape the redemptive, relentless pursuit of God's story, the gospel. The church should be a community of neighbors whose love makes it safe to open our hearts and reveal — both to ourselves and to others — our individual stories. Only then can the living God pursue those who have skulked in the dark. His story tracks down our every scar like hounds track and corner a fox. Joy blossoms as we see those scars beginning to generate beauty. If Christ in the Gospels showed himself to be Lord of demons, disease, nature, and men and women, wouldn't he also be Lord of every scar? He whose scars were turned into redemption, will he not turn our scars into whatever good things he will? And doesn't that allow us to "count it all joy" (James 1:2, KJV)?

We Live in the Story of Joy with the Help of God's Word

Scripture says, "Thy word is a lamp unto my feet, and a light unto my path" (Psalm 119:105, KJV). Christianity is the fellowship of those on a journey. Imagine it this way:

You used to be a slave working in the fields of the Devil. You did his will and harvested the fruit (sin) that gave him his wicked pleasure. But then Jesus Christ came. Through his life, death, and resurrection, he hewed a broad path down the middle of the Devil's fields. When you came to know Christ by faith, your chains fell off and you joined a great company on Christ's path. As you travel, the Devil sends his minions (demons) to the edge of the road. They command, tempt, scream, whisper, cajole, sweetly reason — in short, they do anything they think might persuade you to return to the Devil's service.

Some of what you hear from them seems so tempting or frightening or confusing that you wonder where you really belong — maybe you *should* go back to Satan's fields. Then some of your fellow travelers come around you and say, "Don't listen to that old trick. Here, rest on our arms until you feel stronger. We'll speak and sing into your ears until you can resist on your own." You think this is a great offer, so you go arm in arm, half lifted, half walking, your heart filled with music and words that bring peace.

On reflection, you grasp that all the words and music are traceable to God's Word. One kind soul whispers to you, "I will never leave you or forsake you" (see Deuteronomy 31:6; Hebrews 13:5). Another comes close and says, "Haven't you heard? The Lord your God does not grow weary or tired. Those who wait on him will renew their strength" (see Isaiah 40:28-31). Another sings wonderfully,

> Nothing in my hands I bring,
> Simply to the cross I cling.[2]

Another sings,

> 'Tis so sweet to trust in Jesus,
> just to take him at his word.[3]

As this goes on, you hear less and less of the discouraging, frightful roaring from the edge of the path. Your soul, your whole frame, is filled with more and more rest, delight, and strength. You walk now under your own steam, but you realize that the underlying strength is not your own.

At other times, the group of fellows with you gets strung out along the road. You realize you're alone when a particularly vile, horrifying satanic henchman charges to the edge of the road. He walks along, only a few feet away, haranguing you and arguing with all force and persuasion that you have no business being on Christ's highway. "You are to return immediately to the fields. Who do you think you are, following Christ? You don't deserve that high place. How pretentious you are!" He goes on and on. Then he leans near and whispers, "Your best friend has returned to us." Your shock is complete. How can this be? Should you not join your friend, at least to talk him out of it? As your anxious thoughts multiply, you almost bump into a post, on top of which is a small wooden sign. Upon the sign, these words are carved: "You shall not fear their threats or listen to their intimidation."

You smile at the henchman and say, "Begone! Your lies have no place in my heart." He howls, shrieks, and vanishes. You walk with a lighter step, catch up with some friends, and while rejoicing that God has spoken, tell the story of your escape.

Now we can understand far more clearly the comfort of "Thy word is a lamp unto my feet, and a light unto my path" (Psalm 119:105, KJV). Sometimes, God's Word comes through the community of those on the journey with us. Other times, we're alone, and his Word leaps out from memory or from our own reading of Scripture. Either way, his Word resonates with the faithfulness and loyal love of God the promise keeper. His Word is a constant transfusion of his love. As his stories convey his commitment to us, they persuade us that, because his love is a dying love, it's a love that is undying.

Now, let's summarize the points we've learned:

1. We don't yet possess heaven, though we desperately want to go home.
2. But God is faithful — he makes and keeps promises.
3. Thus we can live with passion, a deep caring and aliveness in light of God's promises.
4. Our passion takes the form of faith: we believe and trust God's promises.
5. Since faith completes the circuit between heaven's offer (promise) and our hearts, hope is born.
6. As hope is established, it generates joy.
7. Joy breathes and grows within a greater and greater understanding of God's story and of how it invites us to unveil our own stories.
8. Scripture is not a dead letter but a story calling every scar in our own stories toward its proper resolution in beauty and joy.

Joy and Freedom

Based on the work of Christ, joy explodes into freedom. How does this happen? Basically, it's as a Charles Wesley hymn says:

> My chains fell off, my heart was free;
> I rose, went forth, and followed Thee.
> Amazing love! How can it be?
> That Thou, my God, should die for me?[4]

Here, joy is revealed as an outpouring of amazement. It's an amazement that's basically a freaking out over God's love as it is poured all over me in a focused, personal, pursuing overflow of his delirious delight in me. The fact that it seems almost sacrilegious to write this shows how shockingly, wonderfully too good to be true the gospel really is. God wants to do cartwheels over me (*me*—can you believe it?), so he allows a death in himself to shoo my sins away from me and make me brand-new, such that God's delight can flood my life as I become the man he made me to be.[5] The only response to this news is what Abraham Heschel calls "radical amazement,"[6] an astonishment at God's love from which we never recover.

This joy, this amazement, becomes so fruitful that it breeds two types of freedom—what I call *freedom from* and *freedom for*. These freedoms are captured in the Wesley hymn I just quoted. "My chains fell off, my heart was free" describes our freedom from whatever seeks to recapture our hearts, enticing us away from Christ's path. "I rose, went forth, and followed Thee" describes our freedom for following Christ in any way he might call us.

Freedom From

"Freedom from" means that our former chains and strongholds have no current authority over us, no matter how great their former power was in our lives. Whenever they seek falsely to assert their old power over us, our "freedom from" their authority enables us to oppose them by declaring, "Nevertheless, God. . . . " Indeed, one of the most powerful phrases in Scripture is "Nevertheless, God. . . . " For example, Psalm 73 contains a long soliloquy expressing the psalmist's discouragement in following

God, especially when he sees the apparent success and ease of the wicked. "What's the point?" he wonders. "Those who hate God are doing better than those who follow him." But when the psalmist realizes he's looking at only a single pixel of the big picture, he comes to his senses, describing himself as having been "a beast" before God (verse 22). "I've been thinking like a dumb animal" is his thought. Then he utters some great words:

> Nevertheless I am continually with You;
> You have taken hold of my right hand. (verse 23)

There it is. The psalmist has made the point "Nevertheless, God has kept hold of me; he never let me go, even when I was being an idiot."

Fellow Christian, please put these words in your pocket to take with you wherever you go: "Nevertheless, God. . . . " They can transform every discouragement, hopelessness, mistreatment, pain, and confusion. Don't believe me? Just look at how you can use these words:

▶ "I am as down as I've ever been. I'm sick of things going wrong. I'm sick of this pit where my enormous efforts bring pitiful results. Nevertheless, God is in it with me, taking my scars into his hands and forming me into someone who can understand the scars in others."

▶ "I can't believe my friend has told my painful secret to others. I trusted her to keep it confidential. I don't think I can ever trust again. Nevertheless, God sees more in this than I do. He himself was betrayed. He will help me find joy in my suffering and wisdom about how to walk with him from here."

▶ "I haven't had an answered prayer about my job in years. While I feel like I can't stand remaining where I am for even one more day, I see nowhere else I can go and make the money I need to provide for my family. Nevertheless, God is up to something good. If it takes him years to put something to death in me so that there can be new life in my heart, then I'll trust his timetable. I'd rather have a belated revival than a premature fall into selfishness."

Freedom For

"Freedom for" means our hearts are made sensitive to the new callings and purposes of Christ. ". . . the old things passed away; behold, new things have come" (2 Corinthians 5:17). Because new treasures have come in Christ, we can use our "freedom for" to declare "How much more!"

A grand occurrence of "how much more" is found in Romans 11:12: "Now if their [the Jews'] transgression is riches for the world and their failure is riches for the Gentiles, how much more will their fulfillment be!" Paul has raised the question of whether God, in turning to the Gentiles with the gospel, has turned his back on his chosen people, the Jews. His answer is a resounding "No!" If God blesses the Gentiles, reasoned Paul, how much more will he bless the people to whom he has pledged his love from the days of Abraham?

From this window into Paul's awesome grasp of God's freedom to bless, we must conclude that we can never pin down the real extent of what God is doing. We should never box God in by saying, "Such-and-such a situation is hopeless." Every situation is subject either to miracle or mystery. That is, God either rejuvenates the situation in this life (the cancer goes away) or takes the irretrievable situation through a hidden process that requires a non-earthly setting for its completion (the cancer victim finds final healing in heaven).

Both miracle and mystery invite us to buy into God's "how much more." The idea is that God will surprise us in the end. Because that's true, there is no such thing as a truly closed door. We are free for pursuing all situations to the utmost, taking risks for God in joyous abandon because we believe that he is up to something so good that, when we see it, we will be surprised and delighted. Joy is the heart marveling at God's daring love.

CHAPTER 13

Part Two Summary

Wrestling with specific emotions requires some understanding of the purpose of each one. I've assumed in these last five chapters that God gives each of these five emotions (and all the rest of them) for his own reasons. The capacity for emotion isn't the accidental result of evolution but is a gift from a wise God who knows our needs.

Anger

In the chapter on anger we saw that this emotion keeps ours and others' hearts from being violated constantly in an all-too-combative world. Anger is the sentinel that stands up and says, "No further with that kind of treatment of me or someone else! Stop and give an account of yourself!"

If we're unwilling to use anger this way, we'll either withdraw or attack. Neither response serves God's purpose for anger. Withdrawal invites further violation of ourselves and others. Withdrawal signals an open door, a green light, a call for evil to drive harder to take new territory. Attack, on the other hand, inflames evil both in the other and in ourselves. Endless escalations follow, as in marriages where neither partner can remember even the next day why they were fighting. It was the fight they wanted; any context could have served to provoke it.

Anger is not meant to result in withdrawal or attack but in engagement — a persevering pursuit of the offender's heart with the hope that repentance will emerge. Anger should invade the offender's heart to sow the seeds of new life.

Finally, anger functions redemptively to accomplish three things. Anger sends us to God, where we must examine our motives; it moves us to hinder evil in others by speaking the truth in love; and it shakes us out of numbness and complacency.

Fear

Just as functional and purposeful as anger is the emotion of fear. We have a deep, primitive fear that something out there is bigger, more terrible, and more predatory than we can begin to handle. And we're right. Satan is roaming about, "seeking someone to devour" (1 Peter 5:8). Denying it only sets us up to devour ourselves through denial, or devour others through using them as mere resources.

Admitting that a real, personal, planning predator is at large is, ironically, the prelude to being unafraid. Why? Because until we name Satan as our real enemy, our dread must remain nameless. And nameless dread must search for a focus. Then anything and everything can make us afraid. Anonymous dread is a recipe for robust, metastasizing anxiety. If I can't name what I fear, or if I name it falsely, one fear feeds on another until my heart becomes a breeding ground with new, baby fears hatching all the time.

Further, in the morass of anxiety generated by nameless dread, my foolish response is to secure my life by making promises to myself (for example, I'll never get caught in public embarrassment again!). Not having the power to keep these promises, I increase my anxiety. I've tied a knot at the end of a very thin rope, and hanging there, I can feel it beginning to unravel with the strain.

Fear functions, then, to show us that unless we trust God and follow him as the faithful promise keeper, we'll destroy ourselves and others in creating our own set of promises. A corollary to this is that when we generate our own promises and ignore God's, fear will dominate our lives. This will be a healthy fear as long as we allow it to break open our hearts, show us our need for God, and lead us to him anew. It will be an unhealthy fear if we try to captain our own ship, so to speak, for our conscience will nag us to admit our wrong. As the old proverb says, fear is the tax that conscience pays to guilt. Fear is seeking to tell us that we have left God's good path.

How do we respond to fear? By turning from our own narrow, provincial promises and throwing ourselves wholeheartedly onto the wide continent of God's promises. We must shift our focus from ourselves to God, who says, "Abide in Me" (John 15:4). Fear is our signal that, in the face of the predator, the only sane response is to get close and ever closer to our promising, protecting Father.

Shame

Beneath shame is the realization I have been exposed. What is so painful about being seen? All too often, in a fallen world, to be seen is to be preyed upon.

Genesis 9:20-27 tells the story of Noah's becoming a farmer in his new life after the Flood. He planted a vineyard and ended up making wine and getting drunk. He was lying in his tent, naked, in some unknown but clearly shameful condition. His son Ham walked in on him and saw "the nakedness of his father" (verse 22) — a euphemism for shaming Noah in some way. Then Ham told his brothers about Noah's shame, inviting them to mock their father. Instead, Shem and Japheth "took a garment and laid it upon both their shoulders and walked backward and covered the nakedness of their father; and their faces were turned away, so that they did not see their father's nakedness" (verse 23). Rather than preying upon Noah's shame, these two sons preserved his dignity.

We are built for a world where being seen is not dangerous but enjoyable. Being truly seen and truly enjoyed is all too rare in a fallen world. Yet, as believers, we don't have to dread shame. In fact, shame can become a great teacher, letting us know that our fear of being seen and judged reflects our desire for honor. Our thirst for honor raises the question "Is God willing to preserve my honor, or am I stuck with fighting for honor and against shame all by myself?" God himself answers the question with multiple assurances that he will be our shelter, our covering, our fortress. We should think of these promises as manifold responses to David's prayer in the Psalms, "Let me not be ashamed" (see Psalms 25:2,20; 31:1,17). In due time, the Lord himself will exalt his trusting children.

Sadness

Beneath sadness is the realization I have suffered loss. Loss highlights the sobering fact that the world is under a curse. All creation labors under a curse as a leaking ship might labor with the heavy load of inrushing water. Everything the ship is designed to do is made difficult by the unwelcome load. Just as the ship's foundering raises fears that it will sink, so loss raises the fear that our lives will sink into death — a death that is immune from God's touch.

Nevertheless, God intervenes against death in the strongest terms, shouting a loud no to death's claims and extending to all of life a promise: "Behold, I am making all things new" (Revelation 21:5). This promise renders death impotent. The promise is like a barricade, keeping an angry crowd from destroying a passing individual. Death is the angry crowd; the believer is the passerby, now safe in the pathway created by the power of God's promise. God's promise creates an opening, even in the "valley of the shadow of death" (Psalm 23:4, KJV), an opening where the believer can face sadness honestly while trusting that promise transforms loss into gain, curse into blessing.

Joy

When heaven's offer (promise) is truly received (by faith), hope is born. When hope is fully grown, it generates its own offspring: joy. This joy is the emotion we feel when we realize that we live in the "foreglow of the coming, promised glory of God" (Jürgen Moltmann's words).[1] The full blaze of God's glory awaits the full coming of his kingdom. For now, the "foreglow" is the dawn of that glory in which believers are nourished and called to new life. Joy — and its more fluctuating counterpart, happiness — are messages that right now the full day is closer and that real life lies ahead. This realization grounds us in a story that is stronger than any story told by Satan, sin, death, hell, chaos, or despair. Joy rises when we grasp that we have a counterstory that's powerful enough to ascend above all competing stories. Joy is a weighty emotion, but it's warranted because we have a story that's strong enough to support it.

So, although we don't yet possess heaven, the story God is telling guides us toward it and helps us realize that God is our true home. This God is faithful: he makes and keeps promises. We can, then, live with passion, deeply caring and vitally alive in light of God's good promises. These promises generate hope, which, in turn, is the sire of joy. Scripture is not a dead letter but a story calling every scar in our own stories toward its proper resolution in beauty and joy. In the gap between promise and possession, the Holy Spirit helps us fix our hearts on God's story of joy. Furthermore, the community of God, the church, through its speaking and singing, helps us keep our grip on God's story. Finally, the Word of God helps us finish the race despite the attacks of the evil one.

Joy tells us that the race will end, that life is not just a meaningless cycle. The course has a finish line, and while we run toward it, it races toward us. God is passionately working to push his ending into history so that he can make all things new. Joy erupts when we attain an open-heartedness toward God, trusting that he will not fail to do what he has promised.

Our emotions, if we mind them as described in this book, are messengers of incredible value. They lead us to become aware of the true condition of our mind, will, and imagination. They help us read our behavior. They throw light on our heart-desires and invite us to think with wisdom about what to do with both frustrated and fulfilled desire. Suppressing our emotions or being driven by them — either way — puts us, in effect, in a classroom with no teacher. Surely our emotions are meant to lead us to *the* teacher, so that we can say with Peter, "Lord, to whom would we go? You alone have the words that give eternal life" (John 6:68, NLT). Our emotions, as I've said, are looking for words. Rightly minded, they lead us to the only Teacher who has the words of eternal life.

Notes

Introduction

1. Abraham Heschel, *Man Is Not Alone* (New York: Farrar, Straus & Giroux, 1951), p. 16.

Chapter 1: The Gift of Feelings

1. Anne Lamott, *Traveling Mercies: Some Thoughts on Faith* (New York: Pantheon Books, 1999), p. 143.
2. Abraham Heschel, *Moral Grandeur and Spiritual Audacity*, ed. Susannah Heschel (New York: Farrar, Straus & Giroux, 1996), p. 31.
3. Anne Lamott, *Operating Instructions* (New York: Fawcett Columbine, 1993), p. 135.

Chapter 2: The Denied Heart

1. Aristotle, *Magna Moralia II*, 1208b, cited in Jürgen Moltmann, *The Crucified God: The Cross of Christ as the Foundation and Criticism of Christian Theology* (Minneapolis: Fortress, 1993), p. 268.
2. Abraham Heschel, *The Prophets* (New York: Harper & Row, 1962), p. 23.

Chapter 3: Maddening Givens and Controlling Moods

1. Charles Taylor, *Sources of the Self: The Making of the Modern Identity* (Cambridge: Harvard University Press, 1989), pp. 369–370.

Chapter 4: The Path to Greatness of Heart

1. George Herbert, cited in Brent Curtis and John Eldredge, *The Sacred Romance* (Nashville: Nelson, 1997), p. 23.

Chapter 6: Desires of the Heart

1. John Eldredge, *The Journey of Desire* (Nashville: Nelson, 2000), p. 86.
2. Sam Storms, *Pleasures Evermore: The Life-Changing Power of Enjoying God* (Colorado Springs, CO: NavPress, 2000), p. 43.
3. Jonathan Edwards, *Religious Affections*, vol. 2 of *The Works of Jonathan Edwards,* ed. John E. Smith (New Haven, CT: Yale University Press, 1959), p. 119.
4. On the importance of having a strong mind, see Os Guinness, *Fit Bodies, Fat Minds: Why Evangelicals Don't Think and What to Do About It* (Grand Rapids, MI: Baker, 1994); Mark A. Noll, *The Scandal of the Evangelical Mind* (Grand Rapids, MI: Eerdmans, 1994); and Harry Blamires, *The Christian Mind* (Ann Arbor, MI: Servant, 1963).
5. Lorraine Bilodeau, *The Anger Workbook: Working Through Your Anger for Positive Results* (New York: MJF Books, 1992), p. 30.
6. Paul Ricoeur, *The Symbolism of Evil,* trans. Emerson Buchanan (Boston: Beacon Press, 1967), p. 253.
7. Ricoeur, p. 256.

Chapter 8: Anger—The Heart's Warrior

1. Victor Hugo, *Les Misérables,* trans. Charles E. Wilbour (New York: Signet Classics, 1987), p. 1326.
2. Lesslie Newbigin, *Foolishness to the Greeks: The Gospel and Western Culture* (Grand Rapids, MI: Eerdmans, 1986), p. 106.
3. Newbigin, p. 119.

Chapter 9: Fear—Warning of Danger

1. Jürgen Moltmann, *Theology of Hope: On the Ground and the Implications of a Christian Eschatology,* trans. Margaret Kohl (New York: Harper & Row, 1975), p. 122.
2. Moltmann, p. 121.
3. Martin Luther, cited in Emil Brunner, *Man in Revolt,* trans. Olive Wyon (Philadelphia: Westminster, 1947), p. 136.
4. For good resources on ferreting out our distorted views of God, see Leanne Payne, *The Healing Presence* (Grand Rapids, MI: Baker, 1989); and J. B. Phillips, *Your God Is Too Small* (New York: Macmillan, 1961).

Chapter 10: Shame—The Agony of Exposure

1. Brent Curtis and John Eldredge, *The Sacred Romance* (Nashville: Nelson, 1997), p. 44.
2. Lewis Smedes, *Shame and Grace: Healing the Shame We Don't Deserve* (San Francisco: HarperCollins, 1993), p. 31.

Chapter 11: Sadness—A Feeling for What's Missing

1. Jürgen Moltmann, *The Source of Life: The Holy Spirit and the Theology of Life,* trans. Margaret Kohl (Minneapolis: Fortress, 1997), pp. 103–110.
2. John Bunyan, *Pilgrim's Progress* (Grand Rapids, MI: Zondervan, 1967), p. 146.
3. Jürgen Moltmann, *Theology of Hope: On the Ground and the Implications of a Christian Eschatology* (New York: Harper & Row, 1975), p. 117.
4. Merle A. Fossum and Marilyn J. Mason, *Facing Shame: Families in Recovery* (New York: Norton, 1986), p. 49.
5. Iris Murdoch, cited in Alan W. Jones, *Soul Making: The Desert Way of Spirituality* (San Francisco: HarperCollins, 1985), p. 143.
6. Frank Laubach, cited in Robert K. Hudnut, *Call Waiting: How to Hear God Speak* (Downers Grove, IL: InterVarsity, 1999), p. 29.

Chapter 12: Joy—The Dawn of Glory

1. Richard Stone, *The Healing Art of Storytelling: A Sacred Journey of Personal Discovery* (New York: Hyperion, 1996), p. 51.
2. Augustus M. Toplady, "Rock of Ages."
3. Louisa M. R. Stead, "'Tis So Sweet to Trust in Jesus."
4. Charles Wesley, "And Can It Be?"
5. This depiction of the gospel seems right to me, but it could easily become unbalanced if the words "he allows a death in himself" were to be at all underplayed. Those words contain a whole trainload of emphasis on God's holiness, his hatred of sin, and his rightful judgment on sin.
6. Abraham Heschel, *Man Is Not Alone* (New York: Farrar, Straus & Giroux, 1951), p. 13.

Chapter 13: Part Two Summary

1. Jürgen Moltmann, *Theology of Hope: On the Ground and the Implications of a Christian Eschatology* (New York: Harper & Row, 1975), p. 201.

Suggested Reading

Anderson, Ray. *On Being Human: Essays in Theological Anthropology*. Grand Rapids, MI: Eerdmans, 1982.

Barrett, William. *Death of the Soul: From Descartes to the Computer*. New York: Doubleday, 1986.

Brueggemann, Walter. *The Psalms and the Life of Faith*. Minneapolis: Fortress, 1995.

Brunner, Emil. *Man in Revolt: A Christian Anthropology*. Trans. Olive Wyon. Philadelphia: Westminster, 1947.

Crabb, Larry. *Connecting: Healing for Ourselves and Our Relationships: A Radical New Vision*. Nashville: Word, 1997.

Fossum, Merle A., and Marilyn J. Mason. *Facing Shame: Families in Recovery*. New York: Norton, 1986.

Heschel, Abraham. *God in Search of Man: A Philosophy of Judaism*. New York: Noonday Press, 1955.

Houston, James. *The Heart's Desire: Satisfying the Hunger of the Soul*. Colorado Springs, CO: NavPress, 1996.

Kaufman, Gershen. *Shame: The Power of Caring*. 3d ed. Rochester, VT: Schenkman Books, 1992.

Manning, Brennan. *Abba's Child: The Cry of the Heart for Intimate Belonging*. Colorado Springs, CO: NavPress, 1994.

Nathanson, Donald L. *Shame and Pride: Affect, Sex, and the Birth of the Self*. New York: Norton, 1992.

Packer, J. I. *Keep in Step with the Spirit*. Old Tappan, NJ: Revell, 1984.

Payne, Leanne. *The Healing Presence: How God's Grace Can Work in You to Bring Healing in Your Broken Places and the Joy of Living in His Love*. Grand Rapids, MI: Baker, 1989.

Phillips, J. B. *Your God Is Too Small*. New York: Macmillan, 1961.

Shores, Steve. *False Guilt: Breaking the Tyranny of an Overactive Conscience*. Colorado Springs, CO: NavPress, 1993.

Author

STEVE SHORES is a writer and licensed professional counselor. He is currently the director of the Center for Biblical Counseling of Hickory, North Carolina, and formerly served as the assistant professor of pastoral ministries and director of counseling services at Dallas Theological Seminary.

Previously, Steve was the managing editor of IBC Perspectives and has written articles for that and other publications including Insight for Living's *Counseling Insights*. He received a Th.M. in pastoral ministries from Dallas Theological Seminary, an M.A. in biblical counseling from Grace Theological Seminary, and a D.Min. from Gordon Theological Seminary. Steve lives with his family in Hickory, North Carolina.

BOOKS FOR GETTING IN TOUCH WITH YOURSELF AND GOD.

Inside Out

If you want a more vital union with God, richer relationships with others, and a deeper sense of personal wholeness, let this book help you discover how God works real, liberating change when you live from the inside out.
(Dr. Larry Crabb)

Understanding Who You Are

Life is all about relationships—with God, with others, and with ourselves. Learn what your relationships say about you and how to make those relationships stronger and more intimate.
(Dr. Larry Crabb)

Cry of the Soul

Embrace your negative emotions—anger, jealousy, fear— to reveal truths about God and gain a more intimate relationship with Him.
(Dr. Dan B. Allender and Dr. Tremper Longman III)

NAVPRESS
BRINGING TRUTH TO LIFE
www.navpress.com